14, 99

D1642598

PINNIE

BEHIND THE LIMELIGHT

THE LIFE STORY AND DIARIES OF A
REMARKABLE LADY

By Kenneth Parrett

Bloomington, IN Milton Keynes, UK

authorHOUSE®

AuthorHouse™
1663 Liberty Drive, Suite 200
Bloomington, IN 47403
www.authorhouse.com
Phone: 1-800-839-8640

AuthorHouse™ UK Ltd.
500 Avebury Boulevard
Central Milton Keynes, MK9 2BE
www.authorhouse.co.uk
Phone: 08001974150

First published by AuthorHouse   2/9/2007

ISBN: 978-1-4259-7245-5 (sc)

Printed in the United States of America
Bloomington, Indiana

This book is printed on acid-free paper.

Mabel Pyniger : 1st December, 1906 – 11th February, 1995

PROLOGUE: LEISURE

What is this life if, full of care,
We have no time to stand and stare.

No time to stand beneath the boughs
And stare as long as sheep or cows.

No time to see, when woods we pass,
Where squirrels hide their nuts in grass.

No time to see, in broad daylight,
Streams full of stars like skies at night.

No time to turn at beauty's glance,
And watch her feet, how they can dance.

No time to wait, till her mouth can
Enrich that smile her eyes began.

A poor life this if, full of care,
We have no time to stand and stare.

by *William Henry Davies.*

Pinnie's philosophy of life;
Oft' quoted when she saw a beautiful scene or object.

ACKNOWLEDGMENTS:

Many people have assisted me in one way or another in the preparation of this account of Mabel's life. I should like to express my appreciation for their help, for without it this story would not have been possible. Among those who helped me were:-

Balmoral Hall School. 630 Westminster Avenue. Winnipeg. Canada.

The City of Winnipeg City Clerks Department.

Mr Jack Templeman. Winnipeg Police Service.

Winnipeg Public Records Office.

Joan Anderson.

Ann Rees.

Nennette Marbach.

Gertrude Waks.

Michael Chaplin.

David Robinson.

Many thanks to my son Stuart for his patience and advice regarding the use of a computer.

But most of all I must pay tribute to my wife Audrey, who in spite of recovering from a stroke was able to recall most of her holidays and other meetings with Mabel both in the U.K. and in Switzerland. She was able to put a personal slant on Mabel's movements that enabled me to write what she was thinking at that time.

I am indebted to them all.

DEDICATION:

I should like to dedicate this book to my four Grandchildren; Emily and Richard plus Edward and Lucy.

Hoping they will enjoy reading about their relative Pinnie.

Kenneth Parrett. 08/2006

CHAPTER ONE

I was born on a bitterly cold day in the City of Winnipeg, the Capital of the Province of Manitoba, Canada. It was the start of the long winter – often lasting some five to six months - the already deep snow was steadily thickening each night. The temperature outside was –10 degrees.

Our flat was one of many in a large block on Edmonton St. and my parents were busy making arrangements for my arrival. All the necessary things that a baby requires had been ready for some time. My mother sensed the time was imminent and my father was sent to alert our very good friend the midwife who would deliver me. I remember him saying later that she had difficulty walking through the snow. Eventually she arrived and I was born at 10.15 p.m. on 1st December 1906.

Little did I know what the future would hold in store. My parents were not well off, but looking back they did all they could, within their budget, to give me a good start. I was to live a charmed life, travelling the world in spite of no financial resources, meeting international celebrities while working for a world-renowned film icon, finally retiring to an apartment overlooking Lake Geneva, Switzerland.

My mother's name was Rose Pyniger and my father, John Thomas Pyniger. I was to be christened Mabel Rose. To put this story in perspective it is necessary to travel nearly 4000 miles back across the Atlantic Ocean to the United Kingdom and on to the market town of Fareham, situated on the south coast in the County of Hampshire. Fareham lies at the head of a tidal creek about four miles long, stretching north-west from the great Naval Dockyard at Portsmouth.

We must also go back to the year 1892 when Rose Paice, which was mother's maiden name, was celebrating her 16th birthday. She lived with her mother and father together with her sister Sarah at No 32 Trinity St. in the centre of Fareham. My mother was taught to be meticulous about the house and learnt to cook, sew and enjoyed dressmaking. The family were always well turned out. They were relatively poor but maintained a high standard of morality and were accepted by the local community as good neighbours. At the bottom of Trinity St stands the Church of The Holy Trinity, where the Paice family regularly attended Sunday morning services. Sarah and Rose sometimes went to Sunday school in the afternoon.

It was now time for mother to start looking for a job. Opportunities for young ladies were few and far between in those days and if your family did not move in the higher classes of society it was sometimes very difficult to obtain employment. Her sister Sarah, who was two years older, had already found employment in service in the mansion house of a local squire in the village of Southwick about 6 miles distant. Mother was keen to look for something similar but not way out in the country.

Monday being market day in Fareham was the busiest day of the week. The local farmers and their wives came into town bringing their goods and livestock to sell at auction. She enjoyed the hustle and bustle of all the people and the cries of the cattle, sheep and pigs. She liked to stand and listen to the bidding. The whole town became alive with the horses, wagons, ponies and carts all joggling for places to park or stop.

On this particular Monday she decided to take a walk as far as the market. Off she went down West St. and into the market. It was always very busy and she enjoyed looking at all the cows, calves, pigs, sheep, poultry and many other items that farmers produced for sale. The Auctioneer stood on a high stool above everyone else with his bowler hat and list of lots to be sold. He shouted for bids, trying to get the highest offer. It was always fascinating to stand and listen. Rose went on through the crowd, enjoying the ambience, passing the Pubs where usually farmers were having too much to drink. She passed the office where the farmers paid for their purchases and looked inside to say hello to a lady who worked there and lived near her in Trinity St.

"What are you doing here"? the lady said. "Searching for a job" said mother. "Really", said the lady, "why don't you go into our office in High St. There might be something to suit you. We have to find staff for our clients when they rent property from us". Mother left the market and went to the office that her friend had recommended. She looked in the window where properties were advertised for sale. She noticed a card that said various clients were looking for household staff and that interested people should apply within.

Mother went inside and inquired about the advert. A gentleman said that they had four clients requiring house staff, all of which were in the Gosport area opposite the great Naval Base at Portsmouth. Mother took particulars and, after looking to see what they were looking for, asked the gentleman to make an appointment for her at the one she had chosen.

Four days later mother and her father were on their bicycles going to the village of Alverstoke, which was just outside Gosport. She was apprehensive about the interview. The house was large and had an imposing wrought iron gate enclosing a lovely front garden. She knocked at the front door and was admitted by the housekeeper. She was asked to wait in the hallway and, after explaining her reason for calling, she was asked to "wait for Madam". Madam turned out to be a very kind lady; she asked Rose to come in and then showed her into the library where she asked her about her background, education and parents. She said they were looking for a downstairs Maid to replace one that was not very satisfactory. She was impressed by mother's turnout and thought that she might be suitable and, after consultation with Mrs Dyer the housekeeper, she outlined duties, time off and wage details. She would be required to live-in and have Thursday afternoons free. They offered her the job which mother accepted; she was to start the following Monday.

Her employer was a senior Army Officer who was Commandant of a large Army barracks, in nearby Gosport, where soldiers were housed for eventual embarkation to all parts of the British Empire; at that time, mostly to South Africa.

Monday came around very quickly and, after packing her belongings in a carpetbag, she set off for Alverstoke. On arrival she was shown to her room. It was clean and tidy, high up under the roof with a dormer window overlooking the garden, the trees and right over the waters of the Solent, across to the distant hills of the Isle of Wight. Mrs Dyer fitted her out with a uniform which she must wear at all times when on duty. She also told her that gentlemen callers would not be tolerated. Mother was naïve and wondered what she meant.

The weeks and months passed and mother enjoyed her work, especially as she could see her mother and father every week. Madam was so pleased that she could alter clothes, mend, wash and iron with great skill. Before long she was allowed to escort their small children to school and to bring them home in the afternoon. She found herself seeing to her employers' personal needs so that a great relationship built up between them. Mother kept to herself when off duty and wrote to her sister about her position and how much she was enjoying it. As time went by mother became a senior member of the domestic staff. She had taken over the responsibilities of looking after the children and nothing pleased her more then taking them down to the beach in the summer to watch the liners and yachts going up to the commercial port of Southampton. She used to dream of far away places that the liners had come from, tropical climates and beautiful seas.

One day mother was asked to come into the study. Madam sat her down and told her that her husband had been appointed to another position which would entail them moving to Camberley, in Surrey. Mother was asked to consider coming with them. This came as a shock of course but she thought that it would be another experience and after talking to her parents on her next day off said she would like to go with them.

Camberley and nearby Sandhurst were full of military barracks; the home of the British Army. Mother found that her lodgings were in a large house situated just outside the military establishments at Frimley. The campus was a very different environment to that which she was accustomed to in Gosport. She was slow to integrate into the new society and needed to cope with the staff in other Officers large houses with finely cut lawns, winter "social evenings" when the officers and their wives entertained, the coming-and-going of horses and military carriages and the sight of soldiers drilling on the parade grounds. Mother was entranced by this life-style. On her day off, she would walk in the gardens and admire the soldiers in their smart dress uniforms. She was too shy to talk to any of them and probably got a reputation for snobbishness.

Mother was now approaching her twenty first birthday and had moved from being a below-stairs maid to personal assistant to the Lady of the house. Among her duties were attending to the two children, taking and collecting them from a private school nearby where she met other Nannies doing similar work. She had now matured into a smart young lady and was accustomed to living in the environment of senior army officers and their wives, in large houses with fine furniture. Life was good.

Occasionally she would visit her parents and see her sister Sarah, who had by now married a local Gamekeeper and moved to a small cottage called Keepers Cottage in the middle of a wood called Boarhunt Common. She now had 4 children, so that the house was always alive with chatter and the delicious smell of home cooking on the wood fired black range.

Mother was secretly envious of her sister and felt that she was missing out on creating a secure home and family for herself. At 22 she thought she was perhaps getting too old for marriage. Romance had never crossed her path. Indeed, she had never done anything to encourage it. Girls seemed to be marrying quite young, why not her?

Returning to Camberley after her day off, she threw herself into her work. One day in July her employer said that the whole family was to attend a funeral. Her husbands senior Sergeant Major Instructor, John Pyniger, had died after a short illness. He had been a tall, upright, typically military man who had seen service in India, Ireland and South Africa. Her husband thought a great deal of him and a full Regimental parade was arranged.

On the day of the funeral mother was to accompany madam because her husband would be marching behind the cortege. After the service all the NCOs' and Officers wives and friends were to attend a reception. There everyone mingled around talking to one another. Mother found herself talking to the Sergeant Majors son together with his sisters. John Pyniger was very much like his father, tall and good looking; they seemed to have similar tastes and mother enjoyed the conversation and was keen to hear more about the family. She could not believe what she heard when John suggested that they meet again. They arranged to meet the following afternoon, on her day off.

At promptly 2 p.m. John was waiting outside the house. They walked into the park and found a seat where they could talk. She was a little shy to start the conversation, but John was not inhibited at all and asked mother what was her name and how long she had worked at the officer's house. John told her that he would be staying in a house in nearby York Town. It had been his father's home for the last six years. As he was the eldest son he would be there for the next few months in order to finalise his father's estate. His original home, he said, was in Nottingham but he had not been back there for several years. The conversation drifted on and mother told him about her family in Hampshire. They agreed to meet again on the following Thursday.

Many Thursdays latter, while they were window shopping in Camberley, John suggested they found a café for a cup of tea. There he told her that he had recently returned from Canada because of his father's illness, he had spent two years there because he had always wanted to see the great outback and prairies of central Canada. He had obtained a position as a probationer Police Officer in the rapidly expanding city of Winnipeg, the Capital City of Manitoba Province. Here he had received six months training and was then put on the patrols of the city. He had met many people seeking a new life in a new country. He believed that service promotion depended on ones ability, rather than on who you knew. He thought Canada offered prospects for any young couple willing to work hard.

He then told her about his Mother and Fathers home in St Mary's, Nottingham. But because of his father being an Army man, they had moved around the U.K. quite a lot.

His mother had come from Lympe in Kent and had died in 1903 just after they had moved to York Town, Camberley when his father was stationed there. John had three sisters and one brother.

Mabel Pyniger his eldest sister had married Mr William Lyver a widower with two daughters who were now living in London where he was manager of a Company called Cadbury Pratt Ltd [now Fortnum & Masons]. He also had a younger brother Archibald, who had married recently. His two other sisters, Teresa and Daisy, were not married.

After a few more cups of tea mother and John continued to discuss their joint situations; mother was becoming very fond of him and was hoping their relationship would continue. John, however, reached across the table and held her hand. He suggested they become engaged with a view to perhaps marrying in the New Year. He also suggested they should think about emigrating to Canada where he had many connections. He thought she would be happy there.

This came as a bombshell to mother who was not ready to make a major decision that would totally alter her life. She was concerned about leaving her secure life-style and venturing into the unknown. She loved the countryside of Surrey and Hampshire, her home for all her life, but did wonder what Canada would be like?

She decided she wanted more time to think about his proposition and would like to see her parents and sister to discuss it further. She promised to give him an answer as soon as possible. During the next week she was able to visit them and they thought that if she was sure he was the right person, then she should go ahead and accept.

John was delighted at her decision, and asked her to accept an engagement ring that had been his mothers. His Fathers estate had now been finalised, and he was the recipient of a useful small inheritance that would help with the marriage expenses.

Mother was now very excited about their future plans and told her employer that she wished to leave them at the end of the year. It was now November 1905 and arrangements for the wedding, in her home parish of Fareham, went ahead. Invitations were sent to both families saying the marriage ceremony would be on January 9th 1906 at Holy Trinity Church, Fareham, where mother had worshiped as a young girl.

John's brother Archie was to be best man and sister Sarah would be maid of honour. John's sister Mabel, and her husband William, were delighted to be invited and they arranged to stay at the nearby Red Lion Hotel, Fareham, together with Archie and his family from Nottingham.

John was busy arranging their passage to Canada. It was a pity they could not sail from Southampton, being so near, and were obliged to book their tickets from Liverpool where the ships mostly serviced North America and Canada. Passports and medical certificates had to be obtained. January 20th would be their sailing date aboard the liner S.S.Oceanic of the White Star Line. The cost of the tickets, second class, was £20 each. These rates included stewards fees and provisions, but without wines or spirits (which could be purchased on board).

Mother was busy preparing her clothes and her mother was creating a new wedding dress. Travelling trunks were purchased and carefully packed with things that they were likely to need in Canada.

Mother's employers were devastated at the prospect of her leaving, she had become part of the family and the children would miss her terribly. As she had agreed to stay over

Christmas, they arranged a special celebration and invited several friends of mothers to join them. Her employer's husband gave a farewell speech and wished her and her future husband all the luck and happiness possible in Canada. He also gave her a reference, second to none. If her husband John was anything like his father, she need have no fears. He also gave her £30 to help with expenses. Thus ended a period in mother's life that she would always look back on with envy and happiness.

On New Years Day, John and mother caught the train to Fareham, where John stayed with his brother and sister at the Red Lion. Mother started preparing for the big day. January 8th dawned overcast with a threat of rain, but nothing could dampen the spirits of the couple. Sister Sarah with her husband Bill had borrowed a horse and trap to travel with their family to Fareham where everybody assembled at the Church. The service was conducted by the Rev Charles Arnold and witnessed by Mary Dowse and William Wing [Bill - William Wing was sister Sarah's husband who was to become the authors Grandfather].

At 2 p.m. the service commenced. Mother was given away by her father George; the best man was John's brother, Archie. Everybody admired the wedding dress made by my grandmother; it had fresh flowers in the head dress. Sister Sarah was maid of honour.

In the records of the marriage certificate it is stated that mother was 30 years old and John was 28 and had the profession of Police Officer. After the usual Anglican service, all the guests went back to the house in Trinity St, where sandwiches and tea were enjoyed and everybody drank a glass of sherry to "the health of the couple". The couple then left to go by train to Salisbury in the County of Wiltshire for a short honeymoon of 5 days before they returned to Fareham, soon to depart to Canada. They could not afford a longer honeymoon as they were saving for their journey. The couple packed everything they thought they would need within the limits of the White Star Line baggage weight allowance. For anything over this figure they would have to pay extra.

John talked of nothing else but about life in Canada and could not wait to get there. Mother, however, had inner feelings of apprehension and hoped that everything would be all right. All the documents and tickets had arrived including their rail journey; this was it!

The next few days were taken up with tearful farewells from friends and relatives and on the 19th January, after emotional goodbyes from her mother and father, they caught the train for London where they would transfer to another for the journey to Liverpool.

They arrived in Liverpool late at night and found lodgings at a B & B near the docks. The next day dawned with wind and rain making their journey to the dock very uncomfortable. The large customs shed was dry and fairly well provided with seats where they waited to have their tickets checked. John estimated there were at least 500 people waiting to join the Ship at the dock just outside. After their tickets and passports were checked they were allowed to go on board. Their large trunk was taken as separate baggage.

The inside of the Ship was beautiful, public areas were very comfortable and their cabin was, of course, 2nd class and therefore on the inside of the Ship and without a window. Their bunks, one above the other, were prepared for sleeping and washing facilities were very good. Toilets, however, were two doors down the corridor.

After about fifteen minutes they had sorted themselves but were surprised by a sharp knock at the door. It was their Steward. He introduced himself and said he would be in charge of their cabin during the voyage and anything they needed, to please ask him. He told them to look at the various noticeboards on each deck where information was available. Meals were served in the 2nd class dining room at the appropriate published times. 2nd class passengers must confine themselves to their appointed decks and public rooms. He said they would be casting off at about 10.00 p.m. that evening.

The couple decided to explore the ship and to perhaps meet other passengers. The lounge was fairly crowded but they found a seat where they could observe other people. They soon struck up a conversation with another couple nearby who turned out to be from Hampshire. They were pleased to find someone who knew their part of the world; it would make their long voyage more pleasant.

The day and evening slipped by quickly and they were surprised when the public address told them they would be sailing in ten minutes. The slight vibrations of the engines told them they were off. They headed down the Mersey and out into the Atlantic. After they had cleared Northern Ireland the weather deteriorated badly and the ship began to roll. People began to retire to their cabins for the night.

The notices told them that due to weather conditions they would be travelling south during the next day to avoid any stray icebergs which might cross their northerly route. The voyage would take about 7 – 8 days. Mother was somewhat worried about this information but John said this was normal practice and there was no need to be alarmed.

Their destination was, of course, New York. Sailing direct to Canada to Quebec, St Johns or Montreal was impossible during the winter months due to ice in the St Lawrence River. The couple retired to bed and trusted in the Captain to look after them.

The next day was very stormy. Strong winds had whipped up the sea and heavy rain made even walking on deck impossible. Many people were suffering from sickness keeping the ships doctor busy. Meal-times were not very busy as people found they could not eat under such conditions. However, as the days passed things improved. The storm abated and people were allowed back on deck to get some fresh air.

The voyage continued for the next four days. The storms came and went with regularity. January is not a good time to cross the North Atlantic. John began to suffer from sea sickness, but mother felt no ill effects. Mixing with other passengers was difficult so mother was obliged to keep to herself. She spent her time writing letters home, as promised, which they would post on arrival.

Just after midday on the 7th day an announcement was made that they hoped to be docking at about 7 p.m that evening. This caused many people to come on deck to see if they could see land. Sure enough, just after 2 p.m. land was visible. They appeared to be approaching a wide estuary with land on both sides. In the far distance was the Statue of Liberty, at the entrance to New York harbour. As the Captain had said they would be docking on time, the harbour was brilliantly lit up, as was their ship. Hooters and sirens were welcoming them. At precisely 7 p.m. they tied up, and gangplanks were put in place. The unloading of luggage took place at once. They found their friends and bid them farewell. Going ashore into the great customs hall to collect their luggage they were confronted with many Customs Officials demanding to know their destination and checking their passports.

As they were travelling to Canada they were directed to the adjoining station were they were booked on the night train to Toronto. They were not allowed to see New York City at all. Mother was thankful the sea journey was over and was looking forward to a comfortable train journey ahead. Seats were awaiting them on the train and their luggage was soon loaded aboard. Mother had never seen such a large engine and the coaches were massive, but warm.

At about midnight the train began to move. Siren sounding they slowly left the station and headed north through the States of Connecticut and Massachusetts. They arrived at Albany where they turned west through the State of New York, heading for Syracuse and Niagara where they crossed into Canada heading north to Toronto. It was not until early next morning, after sleeping in their seats, that they were able to see what the countryside was like. Although covered in a very thick layer of snow, fields and woods were very similar to England. The border with Canada was barely noticeable and about midday they pulled into Toronto Main Union Station.

They collected their luggage and booked into a small hotel for the night. Their train for Winnipeg left at 10 a.m. the next day and so they had just enough time to wander around the immediate surroundings of the hotel before it was dark. Toronto is situated on Lake Ontario and was becoming a very large city with new roads being built in straight lines from the station, intersected with other roads running east to west.

The next day dawned with black overhead clouds and a biting cold wind bringing with it flakes of snow. They left their lodgings with their luggage and found a cab to take them to the station. There the train was waiting; a huge train, twenty carriages long with two steam engines both already belching steam and smoke into the station roof. They found their seats and saw that their trunk was put aboard. The train had two sleeping cars and one dining car, where you could book your table if you wanted to eat in the restaurant.

At precisely 10.00 a.m. whistles blew and the train slowly drew out of the station. A thousand mile journey to Winnipeg was started. Soon the city had been left behind and the train headed north through the Haliburton Highlands which was an area covered with many lakes and woods. On their left they caught sight of Georgian Bay, part of Lake Huron. The hills on their right became higher as they moved northwards and the snow here was thicker, lying in great drifts everywhere.

Mother wondered what it would be like in Winnipeg if the snow continued. She had no suitable boots or warm enough coat. John said not to worry as he would buy these items in Winnipeg when they arrived. The train then continued in a northwest direction through similar country but into the hinterland of Ontario.

By this time it was nearly dark and they began to prepare for the night. They decided to sleep in their compartment where it was quite warm with the rugs supplied. They went to the dining car and bought a light meal before retiring to bed. The next morning they were still travelling through similar countryside but more remote and it was not until midday that they joined the Trans Canada Railroad; the latter going from the far east to the far west to Vancouver. After another hour they drew into a station called Armstrong. A small settlement comprising wooden houses and barns where the people were all dressed in furs. The train took on more water and fuel and continued the journey for another three hours before arriving at Sioux Lookout. Here they were able to get out to stretch their legs, as they would be stopping for one hour. Here for the first time mother saw genuine Red Indians, dressed in buckskin suits with fur head dress, selling their wares to the passengers on the train.

It was not until late evening that they approached the outskirts of Winnipeg. It was dark by this time, so that they could not see anything of the surrounding area. When they reached the city proper they could see a little of the buildings, lit up by Streetlights. In a few minutes they drew into Union Station. John took charge, collected their luggage and hailed a cab to take them to a lodging house that he knew.

The next morning after breakfast they took a cab down Main St where John said were several agencies dealing in houses for sale and to rent. Sure enough he was right and at the second stop they were offered two apartments to rent quite close by. John chose the one he thought would be suitable and they went to inspect it. It turned out to be very suitable, just large enough for a couple. They returned to the agency, where they signed a contract and negotiated the rental, to be paid each month in advance. Occupation could be the following Monday.

Mother was delighted with this arrangement and was amazed at the ease of it all. She could not wait for Monday to arrive. In the meantime John showed her around the town. She could not get over the scale of everything. The wide streets and sidewalks. The buildings were very modern by English standards, four stories high. Most of the people dressed in winter attire with smart fur coats, hats and boots. There were a few motor cars but most vehicles were horse drawn. There was an air of urgency about everyone. The only disappointment to her was that as it was mid winter, no leaves on the trees, and all the old snow that had fallen was piled up on the pavements to clear a way for pedestrians and vehicles. Everything looked dirty. John assured her that all would change as soon as Spring came.

Monday came around and they moved in to their new home. No 152. Edmonton St. situated in downtown Winnipeg. It was convenient for the shops and at the end of the road was a Park. Mother was pleased to unpack her trunk and arrange their belongings to create a home. Putting pictures of her own and John's family around the walls. The apartment was partially furnished, so that there was no need to buy more. That first evening in their home together, they decided to celebrate with a home cooked meal and a glass of wine. Both of them were happy about how things had turned out.

Over the meal that evening they discussed their next plan of action. John said that the first thing was for him to find employment as soon as possible. The journey had taken a lot out of his savings. He suggested the following day he would visit the Police Department to see if he could get his old job back.

Edmonton St was not far from the Police Department Headquarters, John therefore walked all the way there. It was six months since he was last there but everything was the same. He went in to the reception desk and asked the duty constable if he could see the Chief Constable. The duty constable asked his name and went into the adjoining office. He returned to his desk and said if Mr Pyniger would like to wait, Chief McRae would see him shortly. John was a little taken back, as this was the same Chief that was in charge when he had left last year.

A bell rang on the outer office desk; this signified that the Chief was free. John was ushered into the office where he was greeted by Chief MacRae. "Pyniger, well, well, fancy seeing you again. It must be nine months since you were here last". "No" said John, "only six months; if you remember I went home to England to see my dying father". "Oh yes, I do remember now," said the chief. "Well... how are you and what can I do for you?"

John recounted events of the last six months, saying he was now married and had brought his bride to Winnipeg to settle down. He had come to see if it was possible to rejoin the Police Service, especially as he was fully trained. This took the Chief back a little, he rose from his desk and went to a cabinet and took out a file. He perused it silently for a few minutes and looked up at John and said, "Do you really think you deserve another chance?" Look at these records:

Extract from the Police Departments records (obtained by the Author):-

1. 21 May 1904. John Pyniger joined the Winnipeg Police Force during an increase in manpower when thirteen were hired at the same time.

2. 25 January 1905. Fined two days pay; being under the influence of alcohol.

3. 23 March 1905. Fined four days pay; for disobeying orders.

4. 12 April 1905. Fined four days pay; being absent from duty without notice.

5. 30 May 1905. Completed his probationary period; was permitted to resign to avoid his employment being terminated considering his brief record.

John was dumbfounded; he was the only officer not to have completed the course satisfactory. He pleaded with the Chief, saying that now things were different. He was married and wanted to settle down. The Chief considered this situation for some time, stating that they were still not up to full complement, however, he could suggest an alternative; they were now employing "Special Constables". They did not have the authority of a Police Officer, but were permitted to undertake more mundane jobs, also to accompany Police Officers on the night patrols in the city. The pay was not as high as other officers. But if he completed a satisfactory probationary period he would consider him for promotion.

This at least was employment. It would bring in a steady income and he might be able to earn overtime. John agreed to this proposal and thanked the Chief profusely saying he would not be disappointed with him. He was to start the following week, on Monday.

John returned home with the good news. Mother was delighted but asked why he could not be an Officer again. John said that there were no vacancies at the moment; this was the best he could do. He could still look elsewhere but in the meantime this job would have to suffice.

Mother had been busy around the house, moving furniture around, cleaning and polishing, ironing John's clothes, making the house a home. The rest of the week was taken up with exploring the neighbourhood and buying food. Mother had not been to church since the wedding and wanted to find where the nearest Anglican Church was. John said he thought there was a Church called Holy Trinity on the corner of Donald Ave and Graham Ave. He would take her there the next day.

The Church turned out to be all that she had hoped. It was far grander than Holy Trinity Church back home in Fareham. She learned that it was built in1884 of local limestone at a cost of $59.000. Inside it was typical of any English Church but the flags of Great Britain, Canada and Manitoba were hanging on the walls. Almost all of the windows had stained glass, depicting biblical scenes. Mother was happy to meet the resident Vicar, who invited her and John to join his congregation the following Sunday when he would introduce them to fellow parishioners. Mother accepted at once.

With John at work and mother keeping house and meeting other people, the time slipped by. Letters were posted home to her mother and Sarah telling them of their new address. Mother suggested that they send an occasional copy of the "Hampshire Telegraph and Post" newspaper that would keep her in touch with home. She also sent details of their adventures to Uncle Billy and Aunt Mabel in London.

John was able to show mother something of the city. Each time John had some time off they would go to different parts of Winnipeg. Sitting as it does on the junction of two rivers, the Red River and the Assiniboine River, a fur trading centre had been established by the Hudson Bay Company, in 1739, to buy and sell furs and other goods brought down the two rivers in canoes by the Manitoba Indians. This area is now known as The Forks.

Winnipeg had become the chief jumping off city for settlers going west to occupy the vast prairies. The city took care of all their requirements, stocking everything imaginable and this brought great wealth to everyone. The areas round the Railway Yards had great silos for storing wheat from the prairies. In the commercial area was the Canadian wheat auction Markets, where grain was sold all over the world.

The winter gradually became less severe. Spring was just around the corner. The snow was melting and as John had said, after the rain everything looked cleaner. Mother looked forward to the better weather, especially the spring flowers coming up through the snow. John was now well established in his work and time seemed to fly past. It was during mid April that mother began to feel unwell in the mornings and said to John that she might be pregnant. Another month would make sure. As they both hoped, this turned out to be true. The baby could be expected sometime late November. Mothers' skill at making clothes came into full play. During all the summer she made lovely dresses and under-clothes, ready for the great event.

During the summer the couple were able to enjoy the sights and socialising with the local people. One particular lady she found quite interesting was a Mrs Mary Brockman, a Red Indian by birth, who had married a German immigrant and had become a Christian. A great friendship grew up between them. They went everywhere together and always sat together in Church. Mary had been trained by her mother to attend Indian births out on the reservations, and offered to be with her when the time came.

The end of November was approaching and she was getting anxious. However, everything was ready. December 1st arrived, and she knew that this would be the day. Mary came round as soon as mother sent John to get her. At 10.15 p.m. the baby was born. A girl, which mother said was to be called Mabel Rose.

Thus we come to the main subject of this narrative. We have arrived at the first paragraph and our story really commences here. Mother and John were to have a great influence on Mabel's outlook on life and were the reasons she was to make decisions that affected her whole career and brought joy and happiness to many people.

CHAPTER TWO

My early life was fairly normal as far as mother told me. Mother made and dressed me in all the latest babies clothes and when the weather was suitable took me out to other peoples houses, where she said I was admired by all the her friends. Mother herself was becoming adjusted to the extreme weather during the winter. Father had bought her a suitable fur coat, hat and gloves. The odd thing was that when she was outside with the temperature at -10C to -15C she said she did not feel as cold as when she was back home at Fareham. Father said that this was due to the air being dry instead of wet as in England.

The months went by and I continued to thrive and grow; I was fussed over by everyone. Mother was keen to have me baptised into the Anglican Church as soon as possible. She accordingly made arrangements for this to be done on the 17th March, 1907. All her new friends were invited. The service was held at St Mathews Church, conducted by the Rev R.B.McElheran. Godparents were Mrs Mary Brockman and Mr Chas Stewart; Chas stood in for Uncle William in London.

During the next few years life went on as usual, nothing particular happened, although I can vaguely remember the living room being decorated for Christmas. Mother continued to improve the flat buying odd pieces of furniture and father was always out busy helping with the Policing of a growing city. As chief McRae had said at father's interview, the new Police station was opened in Rupert St., where father was transferred, this was in the north of the city where development was taking place. Indeed, new people were moving in from all parts of the world, from Russia, Ukraine, Poland and other Baltic States. They had come as immigrants and were very poor. Many arguments were taking place that required Police intervention. Father's job was to patrol the area at night for one week, and the next during the day. This required him to be away from home quite a lot. I could just remember this period with mother preparing sandwiches for father to eat during the night. This, of course, meant that I spent many evenings alone in our small flat; with mother teaching me to read and talking about life in general in both Winnipeg and England.

During the regular Sunday visit to Church, mother dressed in her best outfit and I was always in something new which mother had recently made. It was during the tea and cakes after the morning service, and in the Church Hall, that people were always congratulating mother on her fine outfit and of course my beautiful smocked dresses. Mother always thought that the new people in Canada were not very well dressed, but she made allowances for their lack of money. One Sunday, a person asked her if she would make her daughter a similar dress for her Birthday, which was coming soon. Mother said she would be pleased to, and then arranged for the person to come to the flat with her daughter for measurements and fitting.

A few weeks latter, the dress was completed, the lady was delighted and paid mother accordingly. This of course, was a useful addition to the family budget. Mother wondered if this could be an additional regular source of income, because since I was born our finances were stretched and any additional income would be very welcome. When father came home she asked him his views and he said that so long as it did not interfere with the running of the house and looking after me, he could see no harm in it.

When she next visited the shopping centre, she placed an advertising card on the public notice board among many others advertising all sorts of services and products, saying that she would be willing to undertake dress making for ladies and children and to apply to her address.

After about two weeks there was a knock on the door and a lady stood there asking if she could see Mrs Pyniger about making her a new dress for a forthcoming wedding. Mother asked her in and discussed the project. The lady said what she wanted and mother advised her on the type of material that would be suitable. She took all her measurements and other information. The lady was to buy the material herself and would return as soon as possible. When father came home he was delighted to hear the news; indeed, two days later father arrived home on his bicycle carrying a dressmaker's dummy!. Here you are my dear, he said, I saw this in a second hand shop and thought it might be useful; price 20 cents. Mother in the meantime had collected many other items necessary for dressmaking and the sitting room began to look like a real dressmaker's shop. Cottons, silks, buttons, bows, needles and thread, scissors and measuring tapes. This ability to make garments brought mother a very useful income during her life in Winnipeg. She was never without work and her reputation for good work spread to many other people.

I, meanwhile, was growing up and many evenings were spent listening to tales of her life in England, while mother was working on some garment. I heard about Aunt Sarah and Uncle Bill, their cosy cottage in the wood, their daughters Nellie, Tinnie and Rosey. I was very interested in their son Arthur, who was always known as John. John was apprenticed as an engineer to a motor car repair company where he learned about engines and had hopes one day of joining the new Royal Flying Corps as a pilot. My mother was always telling me about the walks and cycle rides she took up Portsdown Hill, behind Fareham on the military road along the top that connected the huge forts built to protect Portsmouth from attacks by Napoleon in the nineteenth century. Here she said you could see right across Portsmouth Harbour to the Isle of Wight, all the warships in dock and sometimes, if you were lucky, Liners going up Southampton Water to dock at the great commercial docks over to the west.

It was during these quiet evenings that I would spend my time writing and drawing, being shown the proper way to make sentences and to spell correctly. I found this very easy to understand and became quite proficient. Indeed, letter-writing was to become my main hobby all my life. I wrote to everybody and everywhere and consequently received letters in reply, even to British Royalty in times of crisis.

When I was nearly five years old, mother thought it was time to think about my education; there was not a lot of choice. Primary state education was available but mother thought that it was too basic judging by the experience she had had in her job at Alverstoke. She thought that I deserved something more advanced and as a start mother entered me in the Sunday school at Holy Trinity Church. This turned out to be a great success, there were children there from other parts of Winnipeg including many children of immigrants, speaking foreign languages; I mixed with them all and accepted their different cultures as a matter of course, picking up bits of their language here and there. The teaching, of course, was in English.

I enjoyed the days when our teacher took us round the Church explaining the biblical stories depicted in the stained glass windows. There were over twenty of them, but I could remember each one and repeated the theme to mother when I got home. Among the children were two girls to whom I became very attached. They were the Matheson children, daughters of the future Bishop of Winnipeg. Their father, together with the Rev. Octave Fortin, taught the children some Sundays. I also made another friend who had moved in to a house near our flat. Her name was Helen Howard and she was the same age as me. Helen became a lifelong friend but in latter life was confined to a wheelchair.

I enjoyed these Sunday outings and made good progress in understanding the Anglican faith. Shortly after this time the Church started a full time primary school near to Holy Trinity and Rev Matheson said to mother that I would be a good pupil if she could afford the fees. This was a major problem as money was short already. However, mother said that she would talk to father about this and let him know.

Father said that he had had a chat to Chief McRae about the possibility of him becoming a full time Police Officer but as yet he had received no real response. He would see him again soon and see what he said and hoped it would lead to extra pay.

At the next Sunday school mother was again asked by the Rev Matheson if she had thought any more about me receiving full time schooling. He thought that I was bright and would benefit enormously. Mother said they were worried about the fees. The Rev Matheson suggested that if mother were agreeable, would she consider that if his wife bought the material making dresses for his two daughters in exchange for school fees.... What a good idea, said mother! I think we could come some arrangement.

The following term I started schooling full time and enjoyed every moment. The range of subjects caught my undivided attention. I also loved my teachers who were very kind to me. I was very thrilled when I found that my two best friends were also at the school.

Meanwhile father, in spite of his not getting promotion, was continuing with his Police work. One day he was called into the office and told about problems on the Indian Reservations. A Police contingent was to be made up, together with Royal Canadian Mounted Police, who would travel out to the problem area. There was likely to be trouble and they would be armed. Several bands of Indians were interfering with the settlers working their new farms and preventing fences being erected. Would he be prepared to join the team? It would mean additional pay and all food and lodging found. They must be prepared to be away at least for three months.

Father thought about this at once and agreed to go if it would help his application for promotion, subject to the agreement of mother. That evening John discussed the project with mother and they both agreed they could use the extra money but hoped there would be no fighting to cause injuries. Three months was a long time but mother said she had plenty of work and the time would pass quickly.

The journey out to the prairie would be along the Trans Canada Highway, westwards from Winnipeg to Portage La Prairie and then onwards to Brandon into the Sioux Valley Indian Reserve as far as Oak Lake about 200 miles further on.

The following week, after all arrangements had been made, the contingent set off. They would go as far as Brandon by train. After Brandon travel was by horseback, each man carrying his equipment. Father would enjoy this part immensely as he had not done any horse riding since leaving England. Upon their arrival in the Indian Reservation they organised searches, lasting many weeks, looking for a band of Indians called Beardys Warriors who had been reported to be preventing the settlers from fencing their farms in order to keep their cattle from straying; the settlers were not on the reservation, but just outside. If the farmers erected fences the Warriors would tear them down overnight and in some cases stealing a cow or calf.

Father was pleased to be riding again. His section were the first to locate the Indians and, after an attempt by the Indians to escape, which resulted in several shots being fired, they were eventually arrested and escorted back to the camp. The R.C.M.P. took charge of them and took them back to Oak Lake Police station. Father had not used his rifle at all. The Police were then required to make camp on the reservation border and to patrol it day and night until there was no more evidence of harassment. Father made friends with the settlers and sometimes stayed with them overnight. As planned, they continued this patrolling for 10 weeks after which all the Civil Police were returned to Winnipeg.

Meanwhile I was enjoying my schooling. My favourite subjects were English Literature, Religious studies, Geography and Languages. Writing and spelling was easy for me because of mother teaching me at home. I was at this stage beginning to learn French from other pupils at school. During the course of the year, during holidays, the summers were spent with my two friends on picnics and outings using rowing boats on the Red River. Winters were spent skating on the river and having fun in the snow. It was always great fun to go with my friends down to the junction of the two rivers called the Forks. Here the Government of Manitoba had restored both the original Fort Garry and the Hudson Bay Company trading station. Everyone wore original costumes. There were roundabouts and swings and many other things to do.

While on one of these rambles down by the river, we girls thought it would be a good idea if we all joined the Brownies and agreed to ask our parents when they got home. Both of them agreed of course, and at the next meeting our parents took us along to the Church Hall where they were welcomed by the lady in charge.

I soon found out that the Brownies consisted of many nationalities, daughters of people recently come to Canada to find a new life. I was instructed, by the Brown Owl, the objects of the movement and I was told to learn the "Promise" which I would be required to make at the next meeting. A new uniform was ready for me and my friends the following week. It was a great moment when I put it on and was welcomed into the Pack when I had "Promised" to abide by the rules. This weekly evening meeting was always a joy to me; I enjoyed the games and the instruction I received on various subjects in order to win a badge to put on my sleeve. I was very proud of myself.

What with Sunday school, day school and Brownies, I was always busy. But winter was almost upon us and many more evenings were spent alone with mother, again doing her dressmaking accompanied by tales of England. It was a great surprise when we received by post a parcel from Aunt Sarah containing copies of the local newspaper from Fareham plus news of everybody in the family. I was entranced with the pictures of the Royal Family at the Coronation of King George V and Queen Mary, other pictures of the Royal Coach going down the Mall in London, troops lining the route to Buckingham Palace and the people of London cheering and waving flags. One day I said I will go there to see for myself.

Father was not home during most of these evenings, his Police duties preventing him. I was inevitably unwittingly building a greater relationship with mother than my father. Sometimes father came home in the middle of the night and slept right through till lunchtime next day. I was not able to spend any length of time with him to appreciate his views on life and to hear about his work.

It was some months later that when father was home, he told mother and me that he was thinking of leaving the Police Force because he had applied for, and had been successful in obtaining, a position in the City Sheriffs Office as a Deputy Sheriff, this position would be more suitable for his home life and would mean a much larger income. Mother was pleased with this news and thought it a good move, especially when he said he would be starting the following month.

This new job of fathers meant that he worked in conjunction with the Police and the County Courts. It was a position of some prestige in the community and one in which mother thoroughly enjoyed. I think mother was still a little bit of a snob, a left over from her life in Aldershot. However she still continued with her dressmaking. One day when she saw the Rev Matheson, he told her that they would be moving into a new house as he had been appointed Bishop of Winnipeg and the new house was to be called Bishops Court. He asked her if she would please come and meet his wife to discuss curtains etc. and he was sure she could give good advice. As I was friendly with his daughters she took me along with her. Mother gave advice where she could and we stayed for tea. Mrs Matheson was a woman who mother got on with very well. It was to be the start of many more visits in the future.

I continued to make good progress with my studies. I was quick to learn and my end-of-term reports were very satisfactory. I spent most of my spare time with my two friends, Mary and Margaret. I was always at their house playing and getting to know their father, the Bishop, very well. My mother was pleased that I had found such good friends.

Father was becoming very involved in his new work and was required to be away from Winnipeg for several days at a time in the surrounding area. There were times when he came home and was so tired he did not have time to be with me and hear about my activities. Nevertheless he always provided the things that I wanted, I had no complaints. Mother liked to hear of his work and when they sat around the dining table he would tell us about it. Mother was shocked to hear about some of the crimes that father was dealing with. She could not imagine that people could be so cruel. Mother was like that, she would only see the good side of everybody and I was inclined to agree.

The next two years went by very quickly. I rose to the top class in my school and mother continued with her needlework. Father was obviously getting on well at the Sheriffs Department and in 1914 was promoted to an Assistant Deputy Sheriff at the Winnipeg County Court. Our family was now well established in the City.

I could, by this time, speak French very well and could communicate with my French school friends very easily. This would stand me in good stead later in my life.

1914 saw the outbreak of war in Europe: Canada declared war on Germany a few days after the U.K. The Government of Canada called for volunteers to enlarge the regular army to go and fight in France. This resulted in many people leaving their jobs and joining the army. Father found that because of this his workload was increased and he found himself working very long hours. Late at night, he would call in at a bar for a drink before he went home. This happened many times and mother was not pleased to smell alcohol on his breath. After a few months she asked him to restrict his drinking to when he got home.

I was now 8 years old. The time had come to look for further education. When mother next visited Mrs Matheson she discussed it with her. Mrs Matheson said that Bishop Matheson was on the Governing Board of the new school for girls that was opening shortly at a plot beside the Assiniboine River at Riverbend. They would have a junior section which would be suitable for me. It was to be called Havergal Girls School.

This, of course, brought up the problem of fees. Could we afford it? The old arrangement of making clothes for Mrs Matheson would not cover the higher fees. Mother wanted to end this system as she felt it was beneath her dignity to accept favours from anyone. However, that night she discussed it with father. He suggested that they write to Uncle William and his sister Mabel in London and explain the situation; perhaps they might help? A letter was sent without delay; with father's new position they could afford some of the fees themselves but they needed help.

The fees were $75 per annum, plus $12 joining fee. There would be a further charge for books and uniform. Meanwhile I continued with my schooling at the Church School and was looking forward to the summer holidays. Mary Brockman, my Godmother, had promised to take me out to the Indian Reservation to visit her relations where she planned to stay for a few days, or longer. Would I like to come with her? Of course, I agreed to go.

The village was situated in the Peguis Indian Reserve, midway up Lake Winnipeg on the western shore, a journey of about 100 miles due north of Winnipeg. I thought this was great fun and could not wait for the day to come. We started our journey by 'bus and then they transferred to a covered wagon, pulled by horses. The wagon was bumpy and everything was covered in dust. I put my handkerchief over my nose and mouth to keep it out. The countryside we travelled through was beautiful, rolling hills covered with trees of different varieties, still green lakes and fast flowing clear rivers. Eagles hovered overhead and there were signs of Caribou and Beaver.

By late evening we had run out of road and were approaching the village over open countryside with occasional stands of trees. The village came into view; there were about forty tents erected around a central larger one and camp fires were burning in front of the tepees. Mary found her family and after much welcoming hugs and kisses, introduced me, telling them I was her Godchild. She took her case into the tent and Mary showed me how to arrange my bed as we would be sleeping on the ground. That evening we all sat round the fire to have the evening meal. Sweetcorn and some kind of meat that I thought was quite nice. Afterwards I was offered an Indian made wine. I took a sip but after making a face said that I did not like it. It was the first time I had tasted wine.

I slept uneasy that night and was pleased Mary was closeby. It was a little frightening to be miles from home in a strange environment. The following day we explored the camp and the surrounding countryside. I thought it was beautiful and was really pleased when I was given a ride on a horse without a saddle. I learnt how the Indians moved camp when the ground around became exhausted and would not grow good crops. I saw their ways of making clothes and how they survived the extreme winter weather. They were all so very kind to show me anything I wanted to see or do. Inevitably the week went by quickly and soon it was time to leave. As a leaving party they all gathered around the central fire on the last evening and sang Indian songs. I was very sad to be leaving, they were such nice people. The journey home was just as dirty but I had enjoyed myself so much that I did not notice it. My high regard for native Indians was to last me all my life.

At home the summer continued with visits with my friends to many parts of Winnipeg that I had not seen before. I saw the French quarter at St Boniface and the beautiful Basilica which is the oldest in western Canada, the Corn Exchange and the new St Johns Cathedral. I also experienced a conducted tour of the Manitoba Legislative Building with the statue of the famous Golden Boy, sheathed in 23.5 carat gold, a torch in one hand and a sheaf of wheat in the other, depicting the agricultural heritage of Manitoba.

At the end of the summer holiday we still had not heard from Uncle William in London about the school fees so I started school again at the Church School. I was now at the very top of the class in my most favourite subjects. It was not until November that a letter arrived from London. It was more than we could ever have hoped for. Uncle William said he was prepared to subsidise my education to the amount of 50% of the annual fee and that he would expect to receive copies of my reports and receipts of payments. Mother was delighted and went immediately to see Bishop Matheson the next day. It was arranged that she would no more be doing needlework in exchange for school fees and I could start at my new school after Christmas in the New Year, 1915.

Chapter Three

Mid January 1915 I made my way down Langside Street in my new uniform and wearing my new fur coat, hat and boots, I'm sure the school had Scottish connections because my uniform was of a beautiful Balmoral plaid. I carried my lunch in a new bag that mother had made for me. The snow was at least 3 feet deep and was heaped on either side of the sidewalk to make walking possible. Havergal Girls School was at the very end of the road in an area called Riverbend.

The first day mother came with me to see that I was properly introduced to the head teacher and others. She was pleased to note that the other mothers were well dressed and from respectable families. The school was in a converted large house with additions at the rear. The classrooms were large and contained a desk for each pupil; no more sharing. I was shown into a large room to meet the other new girls who were to be in my class. Eventually we all assembled in the main hall.

The head Mistress entered and everybody was silent. The morning started with the school hymn "O God, our help in ages past". The roll-call was taken and the Head Mistress introduced the new pupils to all the assembled school. I was required to go and shake hands with her right up at the front so that everyone could see me. I was very embarrassed.

Then everyone filed off to the classrooms. I was given a desk and issued with books, paper and pencils. The teacher told us about the rules of the school and said that everyone must abide by them. I noticed that I did not know any of the other girls and hoped that I would find a friend quite soon especially as my two friends, Mary and Margaret, were still at my old school but would join me at Havergal latter.

The new teaching system came as a pleasure. My reports from my old school showed that I was good at maths, geography and the scriptures. At this school I was required to learn every other subject with equal interest, if possible. The future looked rather formidable. Well, I'll do my best!

English Literature was a subject that I enjoyed, reading all the classics. Shakespeare was difficult to understand but when it was eventually presented as a play it became clear. History was presented as an ongoing story about the British people. What interested me most were the details of the Royal Families, their dates from 1066 onwards. I always remembered that mother said that there was a grand statue of King Alfred the Great in Winchester, near her old home.

I enjoyed games but was not very good at them. In fact I avoided them if I could, but not always successfully. I did play netball and tennis.

The term progressed into Easter and beyond to the summer holidays. Going away was out of the question as there was not enough money. Entertainment had to be found at home. I therefore met up with Mary and Margaret and did the usual things, boating on the river and picnics down at the Forks.

Mother was busy helping Mrs Matheson make the Alter hangings and linings that would beautify the new St Johns Cathedral. This took many long hours of needlework and it was no surprise that they became a very good friends. I used her house as if it were my own. The garden of Bishops Court went right down to the edge of the Red River bank and this allowed us to have many happy times messing about in boats and swimming. Our two families became very close.

The following winter of 1915/16 was unusually harsh and I spent most evenings at home with mother by the fire. Father was away on business and some days would not return until late. Mother continued to tell me about her young life in England, whom she had met, what they did and where they lived. Fareham never had snow like Winnipeg! She said that one day she would take her to England to see what a beautiful country it was. Mother was still worried about John's drinking. He had not reduced it judging by his breath when he came home and she was sure he was a little tipsy sometimes. She knew that in his job he had to mix with many people and socialise with them, but there were limits.

In the spring of 1916 Margaret and Mary joined me at Havergal. It made me very happy to have old friends with me. I had, in fact, found another good friend at about this time. Her name was Norah Moorhead. Norah was to be a great friend in later life and was my chief rival in many subjects as we competed against each other in a most friendly way.

It was during this time that I became aware of the terrible war that was being waged on the other side of the world in France. Many men who knew our family had left their job and volunteered to join the army in response to the Canadian Government advertising for new recruits. Newspaper reports were constantly giving details of huge battles and many horrible pictures of life in the trenches. Casualty lists were published each week and some were people from Winnipeg. It was no surprise that when we received another parcel from

Fareham containing newspapers and letters. We heard that cousin Arthur, only son of Sarah, had joined the Royal Flying Corps and was learning to become a pilot. Training would take several months but he hoped that the war would not be over before the training was finished. He wanted to go to France to fight. Tinnie and Nellie were members of an organisation that manned canteens and helped in hospitals. Rose was training to be a primary school teacher. Everybody seemed to be doing their bit for their country.

The war situation meant that father had to extend his work over a wider area and consequently was away from home even more. He always tried to be home for weekends when he would take us all out in his new car. Mother and I never knew how he afforded it.

The year continued for me in the usual routine. I was in my last year in the junior school and at the start of the new term in September started in the senior section. It was during this period that the school was renamed "Prince Rupertsland College". The seniors' school was much more comprehensive and therefore the fees were increased; $120 per annum with books etc and meals extra. Mother wrote to Uncle William in London enclosing copies of my reports and charges for the senior school. A reply was received offering to pay 50% as usual and he happily noted that my reports were encouraging. Mother was thankful that I could stay. She would find the other monies somehow or other.

I had now finished my time with the Brownies and had graduated to the Guides. This gave me many more opportunities to travel around southern Manitoba attending rallies and camps during the summer. I was now so fully occupied that the time went by without me noticing it. What with my studies at school, and Guides, I was always out somewhere in the evenings. This enabled me to meet many new people and I was able to get invited to go skiing in the Rocky Mountains during the winter and became very good at it. I visited Vancouver and Victoria in British Columbia with my friends from school.

Father was spending so much time away that mother was becoming worried about him, wondering what he did during the nights that he was away. She confided in me her fears and wondered what they could do? However, when he was home he was always cheerful and told them about his work which he enjoyed very much.

One day a letter came to say that the owner of their house wanted it for himself and gave them a months notice to vacate the apartment. We were shocked as we thought that we were safe in the flat for some years. We therefore started looking around quickly and found a new one at 640 Westminster Avenue. We moved there as soon as possible.

Almost at the same time father was appointed a Deputy Sheriff, E.J.D. (Eastern Judicial District). Father said this gave the family more stability and mother thought that her worries about him were unnecessary. Father was of the opinion that because he was now earning better money they ought to consider buying a house instead of renting. He would keep an eye out for any reasonable price house in the locality. Three months later father said he had found a house in Furby St, quite near my school. This was just what we wanted, a very convenient wooden clapboard traditional house with all facilities and a balcony at the front. He had inquired about a mortgage and thought it would be accepted. Father was in a secure job and the family were well respected. At the end of the year we eventually moved to our new house.

Another two years went by and we continued with our individual activities. I was moving towards the top class of the senior school. The war in Europe was drawing to an end and one day we received another letter from Sarah giving details of their life in England. Arthur had finished his flying and navigational training and had been sent to France with his squadron; he flew biplanes called the S.E.5. They were the latest model and could fly faster than any other British plane. The girls were doing their same work but if the war ended they would be returning home. Sarah enclosed a picture of Arthur in his uniform and I thought he was very smart and found a frame to put it in.

It was not until 1919 that they had more news from England. Arthur had been killed. He had been flying very low, machine gunning the retreating Germans over the forest of Mormal on the French/ Belgian border. He was brought down by rifle fire and had no parachute. Cousin Rose and her father had been to France to see his grave, which was in a small cemetery in a village called Berliamont in Flanders, France. I was stunned. It was the first time anyone in my family had been killed. The following Sunday at church I said some prayers for him.

It was during the summer of 1918, when I was aged 12 and was working hard on my school examination revision, that mother began to talk about her longing to go back home to Fareham in England to visit her parents and see other relations. It was not that she was dissatisfied with her life-style in Winnipeg but there were times when she had a feeling of being so far away. She was contemplating, now that the financial situation was better, that perhaps they could afford such a visit. If they started saving now they could manage to go during the summer holidays of 1919. When father returned home she put the idea to him; he said it would cost a lot of money but if he did not come perhaps it would be possible. I was over the moon. I could not wait to see this old country that mother was always so passionate about.

We wrote away at once to the shipping lines to get some idea of the price; we wished to travel from Montreal or Quebec to Southampton that was very near Fareham and Mother's parents and friends.

Mother took on more work dressmaking and father put aside odd monies for the funds. I checked our savings every month to make sure that there would be enough.

Meanwhile father, who had been in his new job now for some years now, was required to travel all over Manitoba and consequently was away from home for even greater lengths of time. He therefore stayed with many friends overnight or in hotels and was obliged to spend time with his confederates in the evenings. He was becoming a very socialised person but he was aware that this lifestyle was not one which mother would approve. He knew she thought he drank too much, but this was his job and he had to do it.

In the new year of 1919 many soldiers were returning from France and were looking to find work after their demobilisation. Winnipeg was full of them, during their absence in France, their jobs were filled by new immigrants from Eastern Europe and therefore when they got home they were experiencing difficulty in finding employment. This did not go down to well as they had given their all for their country and now the Government had let them down. Unemployment benefit was so small it hardly allowed an average family to live. Unemployment was very high and working conditions for those with jobs was poor with long hours and low pay, it seemed that employers were taking advantage of this situation to get their work completed with lower costs.

There was also a lot of resentment across Canada by many who thought that foreign immigrants had taken over all the available jobs. The result of these conditions led to a demand for a general strike in cities across the country.

It was only in Winnipeg that the unions were strong enough to actually bring the city to a standstill for a number of weeks during May. There was popular concern that the Police were in sympathy with the strikers and would come out on strike as their union was affiliated to the workers union. The police commissioners refused to talk to the Police union and each Policeman was given the option of resigning from their union or face dismissal. A deadline was set for the 9th June and on the 10th June all Police officers were requested to sign the oath of allegiance to the department and to reject membership of the union.

252 police officers were dismissed for refusing to sign while 22 signed the oath. This virtually wiped out the entire force. The City Council asked for Government help and a large number of Royal North West Mounted Police were brought in to restore order in the city together with several local military units. The city council authorised 1400 Special Constables to be recruited.

Although the strike was well controlled by the union, who asked their members to stay at home and not cause trouble, there was a small minority of militants who caused trouble when a large gathering took place at the junction of Portage and Main Street. A streetcar tried to pass them going southbound, driven by a non-union man and the crowd stopped it and tried to overturn it and set it on fire.

The RNWMP, on horseback, tried to disperse the crowd with batons. The crowd responded with a hail of stones as well as some gunfire. The Police retired to Williams Ave and came back charging into Main St in front of the City Hall with revolvers in hand. Shots were fired into the crowd and one man was killed and another wounded (who died next day). Many suffered injuries in the resultant fighting. The new Constables blocked off the roads so that the Fire Service could extinguish the streetcar fire.

The sudden outbreak of violence seemed to bring the city to its senses and the strike petered out. My father was of course in attendance at the Courts during the troubles and was not popular with the working people when he assisted in the arrest of several men who instigated the trouble. I watched some of these riots everyday, while going to school, and was very frightened. I saw father doing his duty and was afraid he would be injured. Mother was petrified and told me to come home if there was any more trouble.

1919 pressed on and the summer holidays were due. Our trip to England could begin. Mother wrote a letter to her mother and Sarah telling them when they would be arriving at Southampton and they would then take a train to Fareham. We would call and see my grandparents for the first time. I looked forward to this very much. Enough money had been saved and tickets had been bought. Mother and I packed our bags and as soon as the school term ended we said our fond farewells to father saying we would be back in mid September. We took the train to Montreal where we were to board ship, the 19000 ton R.M.S. MELITA. A twin funnel liner that would be calling at Halifax and then directly on to Southampton.

Our arrival in Montreal coincided with the return to Canada of hundreds of troops from France. The town was full of them and we had difficulty finding lodgings for the night. However, the next day we checked in to the shipping company and were shown to our cabin on board the ship. I was very excited; this was the first time I had been on a transatlantic liner. We explored the ship and found the dining room and lounges; we would be allowed on deck if the weather were suitable.

The following day we were way down the St Lawrence River and approaching the Gulf of St Lawrence. The Island of Newfoundland came up on our left and on our right was Nova Scotia where we called in at Halifax to pick up mail. We spent most of our time up on deck, the weather was fine and sitting in deck chairs was pleasurable enough watching the Islands go by. The following day saw us way out in the Atlantic. Nothing in sight anywhere. Occasionally we saw a passing liner in the distance but most of the time we were only accompanied by screeching seagulls.

During the next seven days we had the opportunity to meet the other passengers, and many friendships were made. I was surprised that so many of them were returning home after spending most of the war years in Canada. On the early morning of the eighth day we saw land on our left hand side. On inquiring we were told it was the Isle of Wight, the small Island off Portsmouth. We consulted our maps to see where we were, had a quick breakfast and returned on deck to enjoy every possible moment of our arrival in England.

Very soon, on our right hand side, the mainland came into view. The vast round red brick towers built in the sea, in the middle of the Solent, were intriguing and we could not believe their real object was the defence of Portsmouth in the Napoleonic wars. Very soon the land on both sides became closer and Portsmouth Naval Dockyard was visible with the masts of H.M.S. Victory, Flagship of Admiral Lord Nelson at the battle of Trafalgar rising above the adjacent buildings. I was busy watching everything and did not notice mother standing in a corner out of the wind; she was crying and tears were streaming down her face. She was very emotional about coming home. I went to her and put my arm around her to comfort her. She said she was so happy to be near home.

The Solent was alive with sailing craft and Ferries to the Isle of Wight. The sea was so blue and glittering in the sun. It was a magnificent sight. The entrance to the huge dockyard was now in view and many Battleships could be seen. We were not going into the Naval Base but were proceeding up the Solent towards Southampton. Alverstoke came into view and mother gave a shout. "Look Mabel, there is the rooftop of the house were I got my first job, I can see the very bedroom window where I slept". I had never seen mother so joyful, her face radiated pleasure. This was her home, at long last.

At last the entrance to Southampton Water came in view and the Liner slowed down to almost a stop. A launch came alongside and a Pilot came aboard. The Melita was slowly towed towards the commercial docks where there were at least ten other Liners of varying size and all dressed with flags. Two tugs came alongside and inched Melita into her allotted dock. A band was playing on the dockside where there were hundreds of people gathered to welcome their friends, waving flags and their arms when they could see them.

Mother and I went below to pack our bags, checked their return tickets were in order and prepared to disembark. We made our way to the railway terminus and purchased two tickets for Fareham.

We waited an hour for the next train. We then boarded, seating ourselves where we could see the countryside. The journey to Fareham was short and before we realised it the train drew in to the station. Gathering up our bags we alighted from the train and walked down the platform, "Hello Rose" came a shout from somewhere; "here we are". We looked around to see where the shout came from. Sure enough, there was Aunt Sarah and her daughter Rosey. They ran towards us and embraced tearfully. It was 13 years since mother had seen her sister.

Sarah introduced Rosey who had not met me. Rosey was aged 18 and was at college learning to be a primary school teacher. Sarah said they had worked out that they would be arriving about this time and had come to meet them as Grandmother, in Trinity St., was not very well. Rosey had brought along her bicycle and we loaded our cases on the bar and saddle. Trinity St was not very far so we all set off pushing the bicycle. Rosey and I immediately got on well together and began chatting about our journey. There was so much to talk about.

I took in all the surroundings, it was so different from Winnipeg, every thing was smaller, the houses, the roads, the way people dressed and their Hampshire accents took some time to understand. One thing that I noticed particularly was the tall trees, Oaks, Elm and Beech which did not grow in Manitoba. We made our way down the slope into West St where many horses with carts and traps were being driven along. Fareham had trams which ran on rails along the street but were much smaller than the ones at home in Winnipeg. Mother and Sarah walked behind talking about their journey and things in general. Soon they came to Trinity St with the high steeple of Trinity Church opposite the road junction. They stopped to take in the scene. They were outside an English pub; I had never seen one before; men were all drinking, leaning against the bar.

Mother remembered her wedding day and the many times she had walked down this road. It had changed quite a lot since she was last here. The four of us turned up Trinity St and made their way to grandmother's house. The houses here were even smaller, all joined together in a row with a front door for each, two windows downstairs and two up, with a small front garden. We arrived at the small house that mother and Sarah had been born and brought up in. Mother ran up the path and knocked on the door. It was opened at once by a very old tallish lady with a long black dress and snow-white apron but, to my horror, had no hair at all. This was my grandmother Paice. We were all ushered inside to the sitting room where we deposited their luggage. Grandmother had never met me so that it was natural that we hugged one another and started to cry. I did not know what to say, everything was so new to me.

We all sat down and grandmother went to put the kettle on for a nice cup of tea. Grandfather Paice came in from the garden and welcomed us both. He was not so tall as grandmother and his hands were rough with all the work that he had done on the farms and on the building sites. His face was kind and was so pleased to see his granddaughter after such a long time. He was now out of work and was finding it hard to make enough money to pay all the bills. They had let the upstairs rooms to a couple to augment their income.

After we had had our tea we sat down to chat and it soon became clear that we could not stay there as there was no room. Aunt Sarah offered to put us up at her house on Boarhunt Common. She had a spare bedroom as Nellie was still away.

It was late and as we still had some way to walk to Sarah's house we had better start at once. The journey took us through Fareham centre and up the High St to the village of Wallington where we started to climb the hill, up and up we went, taking it in turns to push the bicycle before us. At the top we rested on the grassy bank and looked around at the view over Fareham and the Creek which came up from Portsmouth. This was mother's country and she was going to enjoy every moment of it. She sat on the bank for a few minutes to take it all in. Going down was easier. We passed a farm with a very old Saxon Church and branched off towards Sarah's house. They came to an Oak wood undergrown with hazel bushes that were used to make sheep hurdles and then turned into a lane that ran alongside the wood. This was Boarhunt Common and Sarah's house was about a half mile further on. The beautiful cottage sat in the middle of the wood.

The house was built of a mixture of flint and brick with a red tiled roof. It had a large garden at the rear which was filled with every kind of vegetables. Sarah showed them into a very cosy kitchen complete with a black cooking range on which were two kettles singing with hot water. There was a large dresser on one side complete with plates, saucers, cups and jugs. The table was covered with oil cloth, in the centre of which was a very bright brass oil lamp. I was shown upstairs to my bedroom that had a tiny window overlooking the woods. Rosey helped me to unpack and showed me the rest of the house. Both mother and I were glad to be here after such a long journey. I was pleased to get to bed that night as I was worn out.

The next day I was taken on a long walk around the area where I was shown where Uncle Bill [nicknamed Bamp] reared hundreds of pheasants for the local Squires winter shoots. Every day we would go to the local farm where we would collect a can of fresh milk and any letters that had been delivered by the postman. One day we went down to the village of Southwick to do some shopping at the small store. I was amazed as I had never seen a village like it. Every house was owned by the Squire and all the tenants worked at various jobs on the large estate. The store had a stable door that was always open at the top, inside were hundreds of jars, tins and boxes containing groceries in bulk which you bought by the lb (pound weight) wrapped in a paper bag. The store also acted as the Post Office.

I spent ten days with cousin Rosey, accompanying her everywhere. It was an experience that I had never thought existed. This was rural living and compared to Winnipeg was a whole new world. When I was alone I began to analyse the two living conditions enjoyed by myself in Canada and Rosey in England. Which was best? In her humble mind Rosey enjoyed a very close and happy family where all of them pulled together and Uncle Bill was a quiet man and clearly loved his family. As for myself, life in Winnipeg was more urban, the city was busy with hundreds of people, my school was very modern by anything she had seen in England so far and the different races she was accustomed to see was entirely absent in Hampshire. I cannot say I was happy with the relations between mother and father, there was no family atmosphere in our house and perhaps it was this that worried me most. I envied Roseys home life.

The days went by very fast and mother said they should move on to London to visit her sister-in-law Mabel and her husband William Wyver as it was he who had enabled me to go to Havergal School by subsidising my fees. A visit was essential to introduce myself; as we had not met in person. The journey to London was made by train from Portsmouth to Waterloo station London, where we took a taxicab to Harley House where they lived. The meeting was a great success. Mother and I were invited to stay for a few days. Uncle William was pleased with my school reports and said he would be able to continue with his financial help. At the weekend he and his wife Mabel took a cab with us, to tour the city, showing us some of the major attractions; the Palaces, the Houses of Parliament, Cathedrals and some of the great Government buildings that I had only read about. This was a fantastic city going far beyond my greatest expectations. I resolved to return at some time in the future.

Our next visit was to be to Nottingham to meet father's relations. There we met Archie, father's brother and his wife who had three children, Joyce and Sylvia and another daughter in Australia, also Daisy who was fathers sister who had a child called Phillip. We stayed with them for six days giving them all the latest news from Canada. I was not unduly impressed with Nottingham but obtained a good impression of my father's background. Phillip I liked very much and in latter life would holiday with him and his wife in Ireland.

Time was running out and it was necessary to make our way back to Boarhunt Common where we could say farewell to Sarah and mothers parents in Fareham. They made us so welcome and Auntie Sarah was so pleased to have her sister with her that we stayed longer than we planned. The day came however when we caught the train at Fareham Station to Southampton Docks where their boat was waiting. The return journey was the same as their arrival; the weather was good and we enjoyed the trip. Both mother and I spent our time reminiscing about their experiences; mother was sad to be leaving her homeland but I was keen to return home.

Montreal was reached in good time and we disembarked, catching the train to Winnipeg the following day. We had been unable to inform father of their exact time of arrival but he knew we would be home that week. At Union Station we caught a streetcar to Furby St. and arrived just after midday. Unlocking the door we both collapsed into a chair, glad that we were home. The house was not untidy after all the time we had been away but there was no sign of being lived in. Father would be home after six o'clock, so we unpacked our bags and waited for his return.

Six o'clock came and went, also seven and eight. Where was he? We managed to find enough food in the larder for supper, prepared the dish and grew tired of waiting. Just after ten we could wait no longer and went to bed. Mother worrying where he could be. Several times during the night she woke to find him not home. The next morning mother was about early, she could not sleep. I was beginning to worry too. Surely he must come soon? Perhaps he had been held up with Police duties? I got dressed and went out after breakfast to visit my friends. Margaret was pleased to see me and hear about my travels. We talked for ages and arranged to meet again soon.

Arriving home later to find mother and father were talking somewhat angrily. He had arrived about 10 a.m. and said he was surprised to see us home as we had not let him know when we were coming. Mother said she was pleased to see him and inquired how things had been since we had been away. Father however, was less friendly to mother, he said that after we had left he had gone to live with his friend and his wife who had offered to look after him while we were away. He had hardly been to home at all. Mother was furious, accusing him of failing to look after himself after they had discussed the trip in great detail before they went, he had said he was happy for them to go. Why go and live elsewhere? Mother suspected that father's friend was a drinking partner and she certainly had not met his wife. Father said he had responded to a genuine offer of friendship which he could not refuse, it was a good offer from a true friend. This was hardly as mother saw it. The row went on for a long time when father said, if that is how she felt he would return to his friend and return when mother felt better. I had returned to hear all this argument and did not know whose side to take. I felt isolated, sad and not knowing what to do I went for a long walk to think it over. This was the first time I had experienced anything so terrible as a family row.

I continued to give mother my whole support and do what I could to restore some normality in the house.

Father came home that evening but the silence was deafening, I tried to tell father all about our trip, who we had met and my opinion of England. Father listened but did not comment. I tried everything I could to make them speak to each other, but to no avail. Presently mother burst out her feelings and accused him of drinking too much, staying away from home when it was not necessary, being over-friendly with ladies who she did not know. I shouted for them to stop their quarrel. I was very unhappy and went up to my room.

The next day was still difficult. Both my parents went about not speaking, father went off to work, not saying when he would be home. Mother asked me to come with her to see Mrs Matheson, her good friend and confidant. She wanted to ask her advice on how to overcome this problem. Both of us went off to the Bishops house and Mrs Matheson invited them into her sitting room. Mother explained the problem from her point of view, also telling her about their trip to England. Mrs Matheson suggested that perhaps father did not like being alone for long periods and looked for company. She said that we should return home a make life as normal as possible, she was sure that father appreciated a good home and would forgive her accusations. She should talk it over in a less hostile environment when everyone had calmed down. I thought this was good advice and urged mother to try. Mrs Matheson said to come and see her again if she wished to talk it over once more. We both went home resolved to get back to normal. Mother and I sat down to write to all the people in England who had been so kind to help us on our journeys and for allowing them to stay in their houses. Mother continued with her needlework and I joined my three friends for our usual daily escapades around the city. Father did return that evening and gradually life returned to normal but I detected an undercurrent of distrust. It was now mid September and I went back to college for the winter term. I was pleased to see all my class friends which tended to take my mind of home problems.

At the start of a new year I was in a new class and studies were more advanced. I found it hard but made steady progress. Mother and father were now talking normally and I thought that it was the end of their problems. Just after Christmas in the New Year 1920, Father was appointed to the Court of Kings Bench as a Deputy Sheriff, with offices at No1 University Place where there was a Apartment for Sheriffs use during late sessions. He was, of course, entitled to an enhanced salary that, as he told mother, would help to pay off the mortgage.

Everything went on as normal during the year. I joined my friends for trips, during the holidays, to Ontario and summer camping on Lake Winnipeg. Mother was happier and Father was enjoying his new status but he still drank a little. Despite this he had many friends around the city, sometimes when mother was shopping she would meet someone who said they had met her husband at some meeting or function. Our circle of friends increased and life was pleasant. My relationship with Mrs Matheson continued to grow and I spent a lot of time at their house. Mother and I went to Church every Sunday and I became very familiar with Church procedures and my knowledge of the Bible expanded.

Three years passed and I was in my final year at Prince Rupertsland College. But the management thought that the name was inadequate for whatever reasons I never knew and decided to change it to Balmoral Hall School for Girls. Therefore I had been there under three different names. There must have been some connection with Scotland as the Balmoral tartan was incorporated into the school uniform.

After the end of term examinations the results were quite favourable to me. I passed in most subjects but gained honours in Matric 2 and Scripture. I received a special prize for general studies and the Distribution of Prizes list in the school magazine showed me coming second only to her friend Norah Moorhead who attained 76% (myself 75%). Prizes were awarded by Archbishop Matheson of Prince Rupert's Land, our very dear friend. A graduation party was arranged where everyone enjoyed an evening of singing and dancing in the school hall. I realised how fortunate I was to have been educated at such an excellent school.

Chapter Four

I sat at the kitchen table with my school leaving and special prize certificates in front of me wondering what I should do now to bring in a weekly wage. One thing I was sure about was that I was not prepared to go into service as Mother had done, there must be better things in the world than that. I was not criticising her as she had had no option, since the end of the Great War women were getting work equal to men, they were achieving important posts in Industry, Commerce and Local Government. Their salaries were higher but still not equal to men.

My friends Margaret, Mary and Nora were all looking for employment, the same as me, and we all studied the newspaper ads and talked about opportunities to suit our respective attributes and personalities. As for myself, I was determined to travel the world; my visit to England had whetted my appetite to see more of London, and perhaps Europe.

I realised however, that I must acquire some training and to that end I enrolled myself into the Success Business College, in central Winnipeg. I needed to become proficient in the arts of

Shorthand, Typing and Book Keeping. My existing certificates stood me in good stead and I was accepted to start at the beginning of the College year in September.

The situation at home between my Mother and Father had not got any better, in fact it had got worse. Mother could not accept fathers drinking habits and was for ever berating him. Many times when she was shopping or visiting friends, someone would mention that they had seen him at some function or bar where he appeared to have many friends and was buying them drinks. I realised I was closer to my Mother than my Father and usually took her side in any argument. I was, of course, with my Mother most of my spare time and at weekends. I could always see her point of view. In spite of the money situation being easier Mother continued with her dressmaking, just in case.

Father continued to be away for many days at a time, not telling Mother where he was or even telling her what he was doing as a Sherriff. Mother was not looking well and I advised her to see a Doctor, which she did but unbeknown to father. The Doctors diagnosis was of course worry related to their marital problems; a course of medicine was subscribed but, as he said, the real answer was to create a normal loving homelife, free from anxiety. She began to lose weight and I did all I could to relieve her of many household duties.

Meanwhile at College I began my studies. Typing was the first subject that I tackled and I found that with constant practice I got quite good at it. I was able to type in the French language and thought this would be an added bonus. Shorthand however, was not easy for me. Weeks and months would go by before I was able to say that I was any way proficient. Bookkeeping made sense to me and I was able to master the rudiments quite quickly. The lectures on etiquette in the offices and board rooms were very interesting.

I made many new friends at the College and the year was going by very quickly. With the knowledge gained I wrote typewritten letters to all my friends and relations in England. I received a reply from my dear cousin Rosy who told me she had become engaged to be married. Her fiancé was the youngest son of a local farmer who lived in the large Manor house of the farm that we had passed by when I was walking with her when we went to stay at for the first time at Boarhunt Common.

Since leaving school I kept up my membership of the Guiding Movement and had remained good friends with Mary and Margaret who were also members. All three of us had learnt many skills and the art of good citizenship. To my surprise I received a letter from the Winnipeg Chief of Guiding asking if I would take over the running of the Riverbed pack of Brownies to replace the current Brown Owl who was leaving. I was honoured to be asked to do such a job and accepted at once, this was my old Pack and I looked forward to my first meeting. There were 23 members between the age of 6 and 10, I was able to reorganise the meetings as I thought in the light of my experience when I was a new recruit. These weekly gathering were one of my favourite times as I enjoyed the laughter and antics of these young people; it also took my mind off my problems at home.

I issued an exercise book to each Brownie. In it they wrote all about their activities. They listed my Brownie programme:

Something old and something new

Something magic and something true,

Singing in plenty, a story to tell

and something to make us healthy and well.

My aims, as I saw it, were:-

1. To stimulate and satisfy the imagination of a Brownie.

2. To learn something of hygiene, Nature and Handwork through play.

3. To learn to be quick, quiet and orderly in a happy manner.

4. To enjoy jolly things with other Brownies.

The book was divided into seven categories, Games, Tests, Magic, Handwork, Songs, Music and Ceremonies.

Every time we partook in any of these activities they would write down how they were performed, each Brownie helping one another. I found that this method created comradeship and the pack learnt many things from it. After about six months we had increased our membership to 35 so I considered I was on the right tract. I continued to be a Brown Owl until circumstances force me to give it up. It was at this time that I commenced to regularly write a diary of my movements and activities.

The situation at home worsened. Father stayed away more often and Mother found that he was living at University Place when he was not at home. Who with? That was the big question. Mother was relieved to find that he was still paying the mortgage and her monthly housekeeping money he brought when he did pay us a visit. During those visits no one spoke about his absence. I was unable to bring myself to talk to him about some aspects of the situation and during these conversations sometimes he did smell of drink so I thought it prudent to keep quiet on that score.

It was during the summer of 1924 that things came to a head. Mother was out shopping one day and noticed a billboard advertising the Winnipeg daily newspaper that gave details of investigations and inquiries currently being held at the Central Law Courts. She bought a copy and brought it home to read. It concerned the alleged misuse of Federal funds and cases of bribery and corruption during the great strike of 1919. Winnipeg, during the winter was for some weeks nearly brought to a standstill by the heavy falls of snow and in common with other Canadian Cities was considering creating an underground rail system and shopping facilities and offices for the benefit of its citizens. The City development Committee had sent out proposals to all Civil Engineers together with plans for this project asking for tenders for various parts of the City. This was, of course, a multi million dollar contract. Notices of these negotiations were all reported in the newspapers, negotiations had been going on for several months. It was noticed, however that one Civil Engineering Company in particular seemed to be aware of competitor's tenders and therefore tendered slightly lower. The City asked the Police Department to investigate and after several months discovered that there was a mole in the Development Office who was passing information that was highly classified. It was alleged that several persons were involved – these were withdrawn from their positions pending further investigations. They were eventually accused and among them was a certain John Thomas Pyniger, a Deputy Sheriff who had been receiving substantial sums of money from the Civil Engineers in return for information.

When I got home on that day I found Mother sitting down crying. She threw the paper at me and said "Read that". I was flabbergasted. Our world seemed to crash about us. This was the end. What would we do? Father had not been home for several days so that we could not find out why this had occurred. Why had he done it, was it all true?. There must be some mistake. Father would not be so dishonest. I was sure there was some problem that would have caused father to do a thing like that. We put on our coats and went to Bishops

Court to seek advice from Mrs Matheson. As it happened the Bishop himself was at home and asked us into the sitting room where we told him what had happened. He was, of course, very surprised and consoled Mother as best he could, promising to find out all he could and left the room to telephone someone who might know. He got it touch with a friend of his who was a Barrister. The advice was that as the police had not finished their investigations that we should wait for the outcome before making any false assumptions as what we had read was only "paper talk" and could be false.

We went home full of remorse and apprehensive about the future, it was not long before a reporter knocked on our door requesting an interview. Mothers temper flew and he went away very quickly. Each day for the next two weeks we read the newspapers to keep abreast of the situation. We saw no sign of Father and I could not attend College for fear of leaving Mother alone. I cast out from my mind any thoughts about father. Was I dreaming all this? Perhaps I was. It did not really happen.

Eventually the investigation ended and Father was accused of receiving monies in return for vital information. He was lucky to avoid a prison sentence as he was only one of a few people involved in a minor capacity. He was eventually discharged from his position as Sheriff and lost all his pension rights. Pictures of him appeared in the papers together with his friends who were also implicated.

It was ten days later that Father came home and I have never seen such a change in a man in so short a time. His face was drawn and haggard and he had lost considerable weight. He just sat in the chair and said nothing. Mother, after another meeting with the Bishop, adopted a position of indifference waiting for him to confess his sins. She cooked his meals and laundered his clothes as if nothing had happened but she made sure he slept in the spare room.

It was impossible for him to continue in this environment and asked if we would listen to his story. He was very contrite and admitted to his charges of receiving monies in return for information, which was easy to come by from many friends in the Offices at the Council. He asked for our forgiveness and even promised to give up his drinking and roving habits. He admitted, however that his income had been cut off and there would be no pension. He would have to find other work as soon as possible. Mothers' faith in her Christianity came to the fore. She said that she could never forgive him for the terrible problems that he had brought upon the family but in accordance with her marriage vows she would look after him and feed him to the best of her ability provided he pulled his weight. How could he do such a thing knowing full well that if he were found guilty he would loose his job?

Many economies were called for and the first thing to be sold was the car. We could do without that. Mother stepped up her dress making again and John obtained employment as an agent for Eagleton and Co., agents for the Prudential Insurance Co of the U.K. The main problem was the mortgage on the house; we could not afford the repayments. After a lot of discussion we decided to sell the house and move into some rented accommodation. We found a suitable flat at 6\376 Ellice Avenue which we moved into as soon as the house was sold.

Our lives were now somewhat different to that which we were accustomed. Our income was more than halved as a family so that our standard of living was reduced to that of the poorest. Should I give up my college course and get a job? I toyed with this idea for many days and went to see my tutor to explain my circumstances. How was I going to pay my way? Fortunately it was nearly at the end of the year and there was only two weeks to be paid for. They agreed to wait for payment as soon as I obtained employment. I completed the course with quite good results. Obtaining a Diploma of Business Studies of Canada, Pitman's shorthand speed of 120 words per minute and a touch-typing speed of 60 words per minute.

It was the practice of the Success Business College to supply trained office staff to the larger Companies in Winnipeg. When I enquired about this facility they agreed to see what they could do. They contacted me regarding a future vacancy with the Winnipeg Hydro Company who supplied electricity to most of Winnipeg; with power generated at many of their Hydro Electric stations situated on the many large rivers of Manitoba. The vacancy would not be available until September 1925, when a new office was opening to cope with the Company expansion.

This was disappointing, as I needed employment now. I told Mother about this and she said not to be too worried as she had other plans that she had been thinking about.

I am going to go back to England to investigate the possibility of moving back there for good. I think we could do better there than here. Will you come with me? I have not yet discussed this with your Father but if he does not agree I shall go just the same. There had been some monies left over from the sale of the house and together with her savings from her dressmaking there was enough to pay for a return passage for two.

That evening the project was put to father. He said nothing. He had no objections but he would stay behind in the flat to pay the rent and look after himself. He made no attempt to dissuade Mother from her decision. Mother wrote to sister Sarah at Boarhunt and to Uncle William in London, telling them all that had happened and asking if they could possibly put them up for a short time while they looked around for opportunities for housing and employment for me. This was a shock to me, to contemplate going back to England to live permanently was something I had not bargained for. Would father follow in due course? Many questions went through my mind, which I was unable to answer.

My life went on as usual, helping Mother about the house and many other jobs that I was able to do. Bishop Matheson offered me a temporary typist/clerk job in the office of the Cathedral. I accepted quickly as this would tide me over until we were ready to go back to England. I continued with my work with the Brownies and spent my spare time in company with my three good friends who were very sympathetic.

Letters from London and Fareham eventually came. Both were long and surprised at father's stupidity; they both said we would be welcome and were glad to help in any way possible.

Mother meanwhile had purchased two return tickets to Southampton, aboard the M.R.S. Mauritania leaving from Montreal. Sailing date was the 4th August, 1925. The day came along quickly, we packed our bags and for the first time I applied for and received a Canadian passport. Mother, of course was still using her U.K. passport. We travelled to Montreal the usual way, by rail, leaving Father in charge of the flat. Being summer the weather was fine and very warm arriving late on the 3rd. The authorities allowed us to go on board straight away, saving us renting a room for the night. We settled into our cabin, which was better than our last trip, and looked forward to sailing the next day. The journey was uneventful; the sea was calm that made walking on deck a pleasure. We were able to sit out in the sun and made the acquaintance of many of the passengers. My entries in my diary at this time record my fears and anxieties for the future; what did it hold in store for me? I said many prayers to myself and hoped that God would look after me.

On arrival in Southampton we took a train for Fareham. There we were met by cousin Rosey with her Father, who had borrowed a horse and trap to take us to Boarhunt Common. Aunt Sarah had a meal waiting and we all sat down in the very cosy kitchen with a lot to talk about. Fathers discharge from his job, our family humiliation, selling the house and me looking for employment. Sarah and Bill were looking forward to Roseys wedding and hoped they would meet Sidney, her fiancé, very soon.

Because Roseys two sisters, Tinnie and Nellie were both married and living elsewhere, there was plenty of spare rooms for Mother and me. Our plans were to visit relations around Fareham and then go to London to stay with Uncle William. If time permitted we would go to Nottingham to explain to father's family what had happened.

August on the Common was very pleasant. Rosey and I spent most of the time together; we were very compatible. Little did I know that this relationship was to last a lifetime and bring me much pleasure in the future.

We spent three weeks at aunt Sarah's house, visiting Portsmouth, Gosport, where Mother worked plus Salisbury and Winchester. I revelled in the history and atmosphere of these very old Cities. The Cathedrals were magnificent. One day I met Sidney, riding his motorbike, he had come from the Manor farm only 2 miles away. I liked him very much especially as he invited Mother and me to the wedding if we were still staying on the common.

It was time to move on to London. Uncle William met us at Waterloo Station and we took a modern taxi back to his house. Aunt Mabel, his wife, made us very welcome, giving us a large bedroom overlooking a park in their new house that they had bought the previous year. After the usual explanations as to the reason for our travels they could not believe that John had been so foolish. They sympathised with our predicament and understood why we wished to change our life so drastically.

The following days were hectic. Aunt Mabel showed us around many parts of London that we missed on our last visit. The old city walls, the Houses of Parliament. But the bit I liked best were the fashion houses around Bond Street. The City simply buzzed with people. When I got home I said to Mother, this is where we ought to make our home. She said we ought not to make a decision before we had completed our visits. Uncle William was pleased that I had completed my Office training, and jokingly tested my ability, just to see that he had spent his money wisely.

Both Mother and I wrote to Father, telling him where we were and what we were doing. We did not want to be accused of cutting him off from us completely. The time went by quickly, each day our conversations with Uncle William and his wife Mabel served to create a better understanding of our respective positions. We were very happy here but after another three weeks it was time to move on to Nottingham. Aunt Mabel invited us to return after our Nottingham trip.

The visit was successful and Uncle Archie, Fathers brother, and his wife took us into his home. They were of course amazed at father's lack of responsibility and pitied us for being put in this difficult situation. Also living in the house were Archies two children, Joyce and Sylvia. In addition there was Archies sister Daisy who had a son Phillip. The house was always busy with people coming and going. All of them were very kind, especially Phillip who was about my age. He took me out and about Nottingham and into the countryside that was very pretty. He asked me to come back some time when and if we decided to live in England.

We stayed for two weeks, but decided to go back to London as Auntie Mabel had suggested. We were pleased to get back to the City, as it seemed more welcoming to me, and Mother was happy too. It was then that Uncle William said that he wanted some help in his office in the City and that if we were staying for another few weeks I could be of some assistance to him. This was too good to be true but, as he said, I might as well pay for my keep. I thought him to be very artful. The next day I went with him to his office, which was very grand, beautifully furnished and high up looking over the City. I was to act as his personal secretary. Next door to his office was the owner's office with a connecting door, and very shortly it opened to admit a tall handsome man, beautifully dressed. Uncle William introduced him to me as Mr Mason (who was later to become well known with his partner, Mr Fortnum).

My training now started to pay dividends; I recorded most of the minutes of the board meetings and typed them up just as they required, copies to all concerned. The general work of the office was interesting and I became familiar with most of the items that the Company sold. I was able to walk about the City during my lunch break, enjoying the pleasures of window shopping.

One day when I was walking round Trafalgar Square I saw the Canadian Flag flying over a large building and went to investigate. It was the Canadian Embassy. Being proud of being a Canadian I decided to go inside and see who was representing us in England. Behind the reception desk was a young lady about my own age. She asked me what she could do for me. I explained that I was from Winnipeg and was working temporary in London and would be returning to Canada shortly. She asked me to come with her to the canteen where we could talk during her lunch break. During our meeting we talked about out respective lives and got on very well together. Her name was Morveth, she was Welsh and lived in London. She showed me round the building and explained what her work there entailed. It was a very pleasant interlude and we arranged to meet again shortly before I returned to Canada. I promised to write to her when I was home.

Mother, in the meantime, was looking around the City for accommodation that we could afford if we returned to England again for good. She seemed pleased with what she had found out about rents etc. She seemed more certain that it was the right thing to do. My work for Uncle William continued and there was no talk of going home. Both of us were happy living with them, and I think they were happy to have us. However, all good things come to an end and during April 1926 Mother said it was time for us to return home to see Father and talk to him about her plans. The Cunard Shipping Company said they had a cabin vacancy and would be sailing on the 3rd May from Southampton. This was very convenient and we took up the offer and arranged to go.

Saying goodbye to all our friends in London was very sad. We promised to see them again in due course. We travelled down to see Aunt Sarah and Uncle Billy and stayed with them until it was time to leave for Southampton. It was a lucky time to be with them we were able to attend the marriage of Cousin Rosey and Sydney at St James, without the Priory Gates, in the small village of Southwick.

Auntie Sarah expressed some concern that we had been away 39 weeks and John had been looking after himself all that time. Did he not mind?

The journey back to Canada was again quite smooth and enjoyable. We arrived in Montreal on the 12th May and took the overnight train to Winnipeg. We had written to Father telling him of our expected arrival.

CHAPTER FIVE

We arrived in Winnipeg about mid morning, It was raining slightly so we took a cab to our flat in Ellice Ave. The city was looking clean and the trees beside the roads were beginning to sprout their spring buds. We were both happy to be home although with some trepidation about having to tell father about our decision to return to England.

We arrived at the entrance to the flats and went up the stairs to our home. The door was locked. We stood there wondering what to do when our neighbour came out of her door and said that she had not seen father for some time but he had left the key with her, ready for when they returned.

We went inside and dumped our luggage on the floor and had a look around. Something was wrong. There was no sign of fresh food and the house had not been cleaned for some time. This set us wondering what had happened. Ah well, there was no alternative but to unpack and make ourselves at home. We set about cleaning and dusting and by evening the flat was looking neat and tidy. Then I went to the shops for provisions. Later that evening there was still no sign of Father. We went to bed about 10 p.m, hoping that all would become clear in the morning.

By lunchtime the next day there was still no sign or word from father. We decided to contact his employer to find out where he was; perhaps they could tell us. I went out to a public telephone and rang the Insurance Co. His supervisor said that he was no longer in their employ and had left about 6 weeks ago. They had no information about his movements. I returned immediately to Mother and told her the news. She just sat down and cried. I was near to tears myself but tried to comfort mother as best I could. There you are…she said, he is up to his old tricks again. You cannot trust him for one moment. What can we do? What could we do? We could do nothing except wait for him to turn up. This was a fine homecoming; our plans were correct, the sooner we go back to London the better.

In the heat of our fury, that was easier said than done. We had no money to think about that at the moment. We discussed the situation from every angle, the more we said the more I became afraid that my life was about to collapse. With a heavy heart I could do no other than console mother and get a job as quickly as possible.

It was eight days latter that father turned up at our flat. He walked in as bold as brass, as if nothing untoward had happened. He calmly said that he had found another partner and had moved in with her at Camden Place. He said that they had abandoned him and had stayed away far too long. Aunt Sarah had also said this to us when we were with her in Boarhunt. Was she correct? Father said they had had no consideration for his welfare being away so long, so that when he was offered alternative accommodation he took it. He told them he had not got on well with the Insurance Co and had found alternative employment as a night watchman with Radford Wright Co. the makers of window frames. He would take all his belongings and would pay the rent for the next six months only. He considered the marriage finished and was considering a divorce on the grounds of desertion.

Mother was dumb-founded. She went into the next room and slammed the door. What could I say, except that I was surprised at his decision in view of the help that Mother and I had given him during the last ten years. Father then packed up all his clothes and before leaving he came over to me and said that its not your fault, take care of yourself, I'm sure whatever you do you will do well and I shall always love you. He then kissed me; the first time for many years. With that he left us. I sat down and cried and cried. I could do nothing and went to mother for consolation.

The next few days were full of sadness and recriminations, asking ourselves if we had indeed been away too long. We had written to him, so that he knew what we were doing and why. Mother, after a lengthy session with Mrs Matheson and the Bishop came home and announced that they would in future look after themselves, both must work and earn enough money for their return to England. As for myself, I renewed my friendship with Margaret, Mary, Nora and Helen and started again with the Brownies. Life for me began to get back to normal.

As soon as we had returned I had contacted the Hydro Company regarding my application for employment. The new offices were finished and I was fortunate to be selected for a position in the main office.

The job was as I expected, dealing with staff appointments, wages and salaries, lots of paperwork for the Great Falls generating station, which was being built on the Winnipeg River. There were lots of other girls working in the offices and before long they formed a club that organised trips to various places of interest. We paid a monthly donation to the funds and called ourselves "The League of Tramps". During the winter we went ice skating on the Red River followed by a small party in a restaurant and during the summer we had picnics out on the prairie. There were about thirty of us including girls from other companies in the city. It was great fun, it took my mind off my family problem.

Mother was trying to adjust to her new situation, she was clearly unhappy, she spoke about father very little but when she did it was without animosity. She was seeing Mrs Matheson quite a lot and was no doubt seeing her husband the Bishop trying to get advice on the best way to tackle her problems. There was no doubt that she gained a lot of advice and courage to carry on her new life. She insisted that I went with her each Sunday to Holy Communion at Trinity Church and threw herself into the activities of the Mothers Union. The church was her salvation, giving her strength to continue with her life. I must admit, it also gave me evidence of the power of worship and Prayer.

Mother set me a good example, her efforts to enlarge her needlework work bore fruit and she was making a large donation to our living expenses. It was now up to me to earn more salary to help mother provide for the two of us.

The Winnipeg Hydro Co was expanding fast, they had bought up various smaller companies over the years and were now large enough to extend their activities over most of Manitoba. The Great Falls generating station was the first one to be built on the Winnipeg River, which is about 128 km northeast of Winnipeg City. It was incorporating the most up to date equipment available at the time, many contractors were working on the site and I was asked if I would be prepared to go up to the site to work in temporary offices dealing with them to see fair play for the Company. I jumped at the offer as this meant a new location and above all a special increase in my salary. I worked on the site for about seven months, coming home each weekend.

Eventually the station was finished and a grand opening was arranged. Sir James Aikens, Lieutenant- Governor of Manitoba cut the ribbon and declared the station operational. I was put in charge of providing refreshments afterwards and I got the opportunity for a lengthy discussion with him that was very interesting. I then returned to Winnipeg to our main office.

By this time I was doing other jobs, closely related to the engineering department and working under a Mr R.H.Andrews as his personal Secretary. I had to get used to engineering terms and expressions and consequently had to transcribe dictation accurately, everything had to be typed in French as well as English so that my training came in handy and gave me an advantage over other office workers. Again my basic salary was increased which was necessary now that we were paying the rent of the flat ourselves.

Most of Manitoba was now crying out for electricity and plans were made for further generating stations on the Winnipeg River to be called Seven Sisters and Slave Falls. This of course, gave me mountains of work which kept me busy sometimes up to 8 o'clock in the evening.

One interesting thing to me was the Amy Street Steam Plant in Winnipeg, owned by the Hydro, which as a by-product supplied hot water and steam heat to many of the blocks of flats in downtown Winnipeg including ours.

Our plans for returning to England were now put on hold, all we could do now was to earn enough money to keep ourselves solvent. As a consequence furniture in the flat was very basic and we kept our food supplies to a minimum. We kept a low profile, so that we were not able to indulge in any entertainment or days out. We were both busy so that we did not miss any pleasure. As for father, we did not see or hear anything from him, he was now completely out of our lives. So far mother had not heard anything about a divorce.

Time seemed to rush by and before long Christmas was upon us. Nora Muirhead invited us to spend Christmas day with them. It was perfect to be among friends at such a time. Mother and I went to morning service at Holy Trinity Church where we met many old friends. New Years day was spent with Margaret and Mary, the day was fine and sunny with the temperature down to minus twenty, everything was frozen which enabled us to go skating on the river down at Riverbend. The park was illuminated at night and parties were going on everywhere. It was beautiful in the snow.

Work started again the following day and as usual I had plenty to do. Plans for the new generating stations were well underway so that Mr Andrews was away from the office for long periods. He left me in charge.

By the middle of January 1929, Winnipeg was under very deep snow and everybody was going about their business at a slower rate. I was at work one day when the telephone rang and a woman's voice asked for me personally. She introduced herself as father's partner, the woman he had been living with. She said that he had recently been very ill and had been under a doctor for several weeks but that in spite of medical treatment he had not got any better and had died the previous day. He had had several spells of bronchitis turning to pneumonia, aggravated by too much drinking.

I was speechless. I thanked her for calling and said if she gave me her telephone number when I had seen mother I would contact her again. I left the office and went as fast as I could home to mother. She was busy as usual with her work and I asked her to sit down as I had some bad news to tell her. I told her what had happened. She just sat there staring into space, eventually she said, " It must be Gods way of relieving me of my great burden", " I always loved him you know, but he made it very difficult, we must organise his funeral, that is my duty, we were still married".

Both of us went down to the Bishops house and explained what had happened to Mrs Matheson. She made arrangements with her husband the Bishop who said he would personally conduct the service that would have to be in three days time at the Cathedral. How thankful we were to have such good friends at a time like this. We returned home and contacted Johns partner who arranged for the body to be taken to the Chapel of Rest. The next day mother expressed a wish to go and view his body. Mother wanted to be alone with him for a few minutes. I knew she wanted to tell him all her feelings and say a few prayers before the funeral. In due course the funeral took place, the Bishop conducting a suitable service in the presence of our nearest friends. Mother was overcome and distraught. The Mothers Union provided a few cups of tea and it was all over very soon. John was interred in the cemetery of St Johns Cathedral. He was only 51 years old. We went home to a very sombre flat. Mother said this was the start of our new life together and when we had saved enough money we would return to England as planned. I arranged for a headstone to be placed on his grave:

"In loving memory of John Pyniger. Entered into rest. January 21st 1929". I paid 100 dollars for this and for its upkeep in perpetuity, but not until I could afford it which was in 1964.

Our lives did indeed begin again. Once winter had gone we began to enjoy the spring, brighter weather. Mother looked better and was busy at work and I was very happy doing my job at the Hydro. It was while I was at work in the office that Mr Andrews came in to say that there was trouble in New York at the Wall Street Stock exchange. Shares had collapsed and millions of people had lost all their money. The Stock Exchange in Toronto had closed pending further developments. I did not realise the gravity of the situation as I had no experience of financial matters. I asked him if this would affect our company, he said it would eventually if our customers could not afford to pay their bills. He said the Company would carry on as normal and we should all wait and see. To make matters worse the prairie farmers had experienced a terrible crop failure and coupled with the depression would not now be able to pay for electrification of their farms.

It was just after the funeral we had a visit from a young man who had worked with father as a bailiff with Hirst & Co. Solicitors at the Law Courts. He came to express his condolences at father's death. He had worked with him for some time and had found it quite difficult to imagine that he had allowed himself to be persuaded to do what he did. He was a pleasant young man and during the conversation said he was looking for lodgings somewhere in the area. Mother said that we had a spare room and he would be welcome to it if we could agree a suitable rent. This of course would go towards our savings for our return to England. James was delighted with this offer and it was agreed he would move in the following week.

The depression continued longer than we had thought and it was necessary for the Hydro to lay off some staff. I was extremely lucky not to be selected. Mr Andrews said he was more than pleased with my work and I should continue as usual. Unfortunately work on the other generating stations was halted pending the financial upturn that we hoped would come in due course.

Gradually, after several months the financial situation began to improve in Canada, but it was not until 1932 that the Hydro was able to recommence work on their new stations. My work in the engineering department increased dramatically and we took on more staff to cope. I was moving around the Company offices dealing with different problems and I became familiar with most of the details of the Electricity Industry. I worked with Mr Cottingham and Mr Sanger who were Chairman and Vice Chairman of the Manitoba Power Commission. They were the two people who had responsibility for steering the Hydro through some of its most troubled financial waters.

The two new stations were eventually completed and the Company began to extend their services to Portage la Prairie and Brandon. I was asked to travel to these places to attend to the paperwork involved. My job was very interesting and I enjoyed it greatly. I was still able to come home to Mother at the weekends especially as our finances were now improving and Mothers life became less hectic. My membership of the League of Tramps now bore fruit. We organised a trip during the summer of 1934 to British Columbia visiting Vancouver, Victoria and the Butchart Gardens. Staying with friends of ours, Mr and Mrs Fenton and their daughter, Violet, in Vancouver and at the Glenshiel Hotel in Victoria. On the way home we stayed for two nights in Banff, Alberta. We returned to Winnipeg after three weeks of the best holiday I had had for a long time.

1933 and 1934 passed in the same fashion, working hard and having outings with my friends. Occasionally I was able take Mother with me which she enjoyed very much. Christmas day 1934 we spent at home; Church in the morning followed by a lovely lunch that mother prepared. We read all the Christmas cards that had come from England and our other friends in Canada, we then opened our presents to each other. That day I sat down and recorded in my diaries all that had happened during this year and my innermost thoughts; I would soon be leaving Canada for good and this troubled me a lot. I would always discuss this with Margaret when we were together; she never failed to encourage me to think positive, everything was sure to be OK.

Spring 1935 came along, bringing better than usual weather. I was able to visit Helens house that had a lovely garden complete with a log cabin. We were able to visit many other places of interest, such as Camp Morton, Assiniboine Park and Pavilion and the Legislative Building to see and hear the Members in session.

Mother continued her dress making but during the summer she seemed to be living in another world, she seemed far away, she talked very little and I thought began to age a little. She was 54 years old. Her health was not all that it should have been, she suffered with throat problems and was always visiting the Doctor for medication.

It was during August that Mother brought up the question of returning to England. She said that it was her dearest wish to return to her roots for the rest of her life. She had written to Aunt Mabel in London, telling her about father's death and her wish to return as soon as possible. Aunt Mabel offered to put them up for a short time, if they came, while we looked for a flat and I found employment. We talked about this for some days, discussing the pros and cons of such a move. The biggest problem was that I had now worked myself up to a senior position in the Hydro offices. My job was secure and my present salary was higher than most at my level. I had been with them for ten years and had now qualified for a pension. Should I give all this up?

It had been my hobby to write to people who were affecting our lives, and during the year I had written to Queen Mary at Buckingham Palace, London, expressing my concern about the Kings illness, hoping that his health would soon improve. It was with great concern that I heard that he had passed away and straight away I sent my condolences to the Palace. There was now a new King. The Prince of Wales had now become King Edward VIII. Eventually I received a reply from a secretary on behalf of the Queen Mary thanking me for my concern. This gave me confidence to write another letter to the new King congratulating him on his accession, saying I was sure the people of Canada would wish him great happiness.

The discussions with mother about our leaving continued, but Mothers resolve did not diminish. I gradually began to accept the situation that it was inevitable that we should go. When I could see that the decision was irreversible I geared myself up to informing my employers. At the end of August I told Mr Andrews of my decision to go with my Mother back to England, on account of her health. I said I would like to leave at the end of September.

I realised that they did not like me leaving and expressed surprise at my decision. However they understood my situation and wished me all the luck in the world. All the senior Directors said they would give me references.

References: quoted verbatim from the originals -

From S.P.Matheson. Archbishop of Rupert's Land and Primate of all Canada.

91. Kingsway. Winnipeg. Canada. 18.9.35.

To whom it may concern.

I have pleasure in certifying that Miss Mabel Pynigar is well known to me and has been all her life. It is a pleasure also to me to testify to her excellent character and attractive personality. She was educated in the Church School in Winnipeg where she made for herself a fine record in Scholarship. After leaving School she entered one of our Civic Offices as a Secretary and Stenographer, where she has remained ever since, some nine years. There she has done extremely good work to their utmost satisfaction. She now goes on a somewhat prolonged holiday to England. I very warmly recommend her as a much competent and useful girl and one who will be most loyal to any duty that she may undertake.

Signed by the Archbishop

From R.H.Andrews. Electrical Engineer. City of Winnipeg
Hydro Electric System.

55-57-59. Princess St. Winnipeg. Manitoba. Canada.

28.9.35.

To whom it may concern.

*The bearer, Miss M.R.Pyniger, has been employed by the City of
Winnipeg Hydro Electric System since 1926, and has been the Chief
Engineers Secretary since 1927. In addition to this secretarial work she has
taken dictation from several members of the Engineering staff which had
involved technical reports, tabulation of technical data and other such work
as is incident to an Engineering office.*

*Miss Pyniger has done all my work since 1927, and I am very pleased
to be able to state that her work has been satisfactory in every way. I have
no hesitation in recommending her for a position involving secretarial work
or special work involving dictation and typing of engineering data, reports
etc. It is generally recognized that engineering dictation is very difficult due
to the terms and expressions used, consequently her ability to accurately
transcribe dictation of this kind had resulted from a sound training.*

*I shall be most pleased to furnish any additional information that may
be required.*

Signed by R.H.Andrews.

From J.G.Glassco. Manager; City of Winnipeg Hydro Electric
System.

55-57-59. Princess St. Winnipeg.

September 21st 1935.

To whom it may concern.

This is to certify that Miss M.Pyniger has been in the employ of the Hydro Electric System of the City of Winnipeg as a secretary and stenographer for the engineering Department for the last eleven years, she is leaving of her own accord to live in England on account of her Mothers health.

We regret very much her leaving our service and can heartily recommend her to anyone needing a competent stenographer, particularly one who is thoroughly qualified for an engineering office.

Signed by J.G.Glassco.

From Mr W. Sawyer. Chief Engineer. Hydro Electric System.

September 21st 1935.

To whom it may concern.

Dear Sir.

This is to certify that Miss M.R.Pyniger has been employed by the City of Winnipeg Hydro System for the past ten years as Secretary to the Chief Engineer. The duties of this position require special competency in engineering specifications and technical correspondence. I have no hesitation in saying that Miss Pyniger has performed her satisfactory in every respect.

We cannot give any better recommendation than to say that we would welcome the opportunity of re-engaging Miss Pyniger if she should desire to return to Canada.

Yours truly,

W.Sawyer.

It was a foregone conclusion that when Mother had purchased the tickets we would be leaving Canada, perhaps during mid-September when we expected the tickets to arrive. One way, of course! This brought home to me the fact that I would soon be leaving all my friends and above all the Land of my Birth. I was proud of being a Canadian. When I told my friends that we would be going to live in England all of them were genuinely sorry; I promised I would write as often as possible. I wrote to cousin Rosey, in England, who was now living on a farm near the Village of Southwick, about seven miles from the City of Portsmouth. She now had two sons, Peter and Kenneth and I was looking forward to seeing them.

We now set about getting rid of all our furniture and other things that we could not take with us. James, our lodger wanted to take over our flat and asked if he could buy most of the furniture, we agreed a price which helped us a lot.

At the end of September my best friends organised a farewell party for both of us. Everyone we knew was invited. It was held in the meeting hall at the Holy Trinity Church. Bishop Matheson gave a small speech to which I was asked to respond. It was the most tearful period for me. I loved them all. I promised them if I ever returned I would visit them wherever they were.

October 2nd 1935 saw us boarding the train at Winnipeg Central Station bound for Montreal where our Boat awaited. We had bought a trunk in which we managed to pack most of our dearest belongings, beside which we each carried a case with our personal things for the voyage. We arrived at the docks late on the 3rd and went aboard the S.S.Montcalm; a very modern boat, with every comfort. We were due to sail on the 4th and at about 9.a.m. there was a knock on our cabin door and who should it be but Nora Muirhead who was in Montreal at the time and decided to come and see us off. What a good friend she was!

Nora stayed with us on board for the remainder of the day. She was the last of my best friends I was to see in Canada; after she left us we went back to our cabin where I realised this was the final hour in my Country. I wept, with Mother trying to console me. I could not bear to be on deck when we departed, so I went to bed and tried to sleep.

I awoke early next morning to the sound of the crew hurrying along the corridors and the steady hum of the engines. Our cabin had no windows so that I dressed quickly and went up the stairway where I could see out. I could see we were still in the St Lawrence River, but a long way down stream as the shorelines were far away. I went down and told Mother we were well on our way. After breakfast we both went on deck and found a spot that was out of the wind to sit and watch; it was here that we met Dr Richards and his wife and daughter, who were returning to England after a lengthy stay in Ontario. We made friends with them and most times dined together. It was not very long before the Mainland of Canada disappeared and the Islands of Nova Scotia and Newfoundland came into view on the horizon. We were now well into the Gulf of St Lawrence. Late in the afternoon all land disappeared and we headed out into the Atlantic Ocean.

My early life, my work, my friends, and my Father, all flashed through my mind as I stood in the wind looking out to sea. I was heading for a new life, where would I be next year this time? Where would I be living? I said a quiet prayer and returned to Mother.

CHAPTER SIX

This morning, October 11th, after seven days at sea, mother and I went up to the dining room for breakfast. It was fairly crowded but Dr Richards had found a table and was waiting for us. There was a distinctly different atmosphere over the whole dining room. People were chatting to one another in louder voices than usual as this would be one of their last days aboard and they busied themselves consolidating their friendships, promising to keep in touch.

Away to the south we could see the French coast and the outline of Le Harve harbour. It was announced that we would not be going into the harbour but would anchor outside to drop off passengers bound for Paris etc. This took about four hours and we were soon on our way north to Southampton.

The English Channel was very busy with various ships going East and West. Our ship, S.S. Montcalm, made her way safely through the traffic, We were surprised to see so many naval ships making their way in our direction. Passengers were speculating about this busy movement of warships. The newspapers that we had seen on board were full of the German re-armament; was this anything to do with that?

Late afternoon we entered the approaches to Portsmouth Harbour, the Isle of Wight was on our left, which looked beautiful with two small seaside towns in the bays flanked by high cliffs. In the outer approaches to this part of the harbour, called the Solent, were the huge red brick round forts built in the middle of the sea to repel any Napoleonic invasion of England. Once we were past these there appeared a sight that I shall never forget. As far as the eye could see to the west there were Naval warships of all types, all anchored in line, flying their flags and ensigns. My estimate was that there around two hundred ships. This prompted the passengers to crowd the top decks to get the best view of this great display of Naval might. What was it all in aid of?

The ship carefully made her way through all this traffic towards Southampton docks, a good ten miles further on. It was not long before the reason for this display became clear, the new King, Edward V111 was to inspect the fleet the following week; hence all the preparations but really it was a political move to show any aggressor the strength of the United Kingdoms naval power.

Our ship made its way slowly towards Southampton docks and before long two tugs came and took us in tow, carefully nudging us into the allocated dock. A military band was playing, welcoming us to England. Porters, crew, dockyard workers and security police were busy about their duties. Cranes, trains, taxis and lorries, all busy loading and unloading. Alongside the Montcalm were at least ten other liners of varying sizes. Flying the flags of the Cunard and P & O lines plus others I did not recognise. It was indeed a very busy port.

Mother and I went ashore after saying our farewells to the Richards family and other people that we had met on board. Our finances allowed us to hire a taxi to take us to Boarhunt Common, where auntie Sarah and uncle Bill were waiting to greet us. Mother was in tears as she hugged her sister, she was so happy to be home. They made us welcome to their cottage which since all their daughters had left home had been altered into two cottages. But it was still large enough for all four of us.

All three girls had now married and were living quite close. Tinnie had married another gamekeeper, Fred Crook. Nellie had married a very skilled gardener and thatcher, John Read. Rose, as I have already said married a local farmer, Sydney Parrett. The sitting room was hung with pictures of their son John, in RFC uniform who had been killed in the First World War, in France.

The October winds were creating havoc with the trees in the woods surrounding the cottage, limbs were broken off and leaves covered the ground. Autumn had arrived with a vengeance. We made up the fire and closed all the doors to make ourselves as cosy as possible, all four of us had a lot to talk about our past experiences since we had last met. The time went by fast and before long it was midnight. Mother told her story about father and his escapades leading to his death. Aunt Sarah [now called Ginnie by all her family] related the details of the three weddings and Bamp and Rosys visit to France to see their sons Johns grave on the French/Belgian border at a small village of Berliamont in the forest of Mormal. They had taken many photographs and had brought home a brass figure of the Virgin Mary that they had found upon his grave, put there no doubt by thankful local people [this is still in the ownership of the Author].

Both of us were pleased to go up to bed that night. The room was cosy with a small window overlooking the woods. We slept well. I brought my diary up to date with the many things that I had seen during the last few days.

The next morning both of us went down to breakfast, the smell of bacon and eggs cooking on the range was delicious, the tea was hot and strong, we finished with hot toasted home-made bread, butter and marmalade. Never had I tasted such a lovely meal.

Ginnie suggested the three women went for a walk across the common to visit Rosie and her two children, the rain and wind had eased which made our walk possible, it was not far to the farm but Mother and Ginnie talked endlessly but eventually we arrived. After going in the house we embraced our relatives, especially the two young boys. Sidney was out on the farm somewhere, so we did not see him. Rosie suggested that after the Fleet Review the following week all of us should go up to the top of Portsdown Hill overlooking the harbour where we would get a good view of the illuminated warships after dark. We jumped at this suggestion and agreed to meet at a suitable point near to a tall memorial to Admiral Nelson.

The next day was Sunday and mother and I asked if we could attend a service at the local Church at South Boarhunt. We had not been to Church for several weeks and we both felt we needed some spiritual blessing and to partake in Holy Communion. We wished to thank God for our safe journey to England and his guidance for our future.

St Nicholas Church, surrounded by ancient yew trees, was one of the oldest Saxon Churches in England. I thought it was wonderful but very small compared to the new Churches in Canada. On the wall inside was a plaque in memory of Ginnies son John and a fellow soldier, who was killed about the same time. Ginnie took some flowers to arrange around the plaque. The Church was so small it was unbelievable but the service was very nice; we both felt better for it. Among the congregation were several members of the Parrett family, who all sat in their special box pew; they all lived at Manor farm very near the Church. Sidney's father was a very small man, who reminded me of pictures I had seen of the South African General Smuts with a small pointed beard, he insisted that his family attended Church regularly.

Mother, after only a few days in England, was looking decidedly better. She seemed happy, which I had not seen for ages. It was now time for me to write to all my friends in Canada, telling them of our adventures. I spent most of the following day busily doing just that.

The following Monday Uncle Bill came home with some great news, he had obtained some tickets supplied by his employer to go aboard a ship from Portsmouth Harbour which would follow the Royal Yacht during the new Kings inspection of the fleet. We had to be at the docks at 6,00 a.m. We were all excited and arranged a taxi to take us there in good time. The fleet review took place and our ship followed at a discreet distance behind the Royal Yacht. We were so lucky and took many photographs. Everybody was in high spirits and we were all tired out when we returned to Portsmouth after being at sea for about 5 hours. The illuminations were due the following day and we all walked to the top of Portsdown hill to a spot around a monument to Admiral Lord Nelson. We sat upon the stonework to await the illuminations. At precisely 9 pm the lights came on. Every ship that we had seen the previous day was alight from stem to stern, a magnificent sight, it almost lit up where we were seated which was about 6 miles away. Ginnie had brought some sandwiches and hot tea in a flask. Uncle bill had brought something a bit stronger in a silver flask. What an evening!!

During the following weeks we visited Nellie and John and Tinnie and Fred. But most important was that we were able to unwind in a kind and stable family atmosphere, savouring the quietness on the countryside. As for me, I was happy for mother but after a few weeks I began to wonder where all this would leave me, I had a future too! I began to feel I ought to move on. Mother however wanted to visit other parts of the

Country, so that if Auntie Ginnie was happy for us to stay we should do it now that we were so near to the places she wanted to go.

In private I told mother how I felt, she understood but still wanted to stay a little longer. We therefore visited Salisbury where mother had her honeymoon. We found the hotel without much trouble and visited the wonderful Cathedral that had the highest spire in England. While in this part of Wiltshire we went on to Whaddon, a village near Melksham, where Nellie's husband John had an Uncle Tom and Aunt Eliza. We stayed there two days and had a ride in Uncle Tom's dog cart pulled by a very fast pony. We then returned to Salisbury and back to Fareham by train and on to Boarhunt Common.

It was here that the next day Rosie and Sidney came to see us with the news that they had sold up their farm and were moving over Portsdown Hill to the large village of Portchester where they had bought a small business. It was called the Old Oak Dairy. There in the main street was a red brick house with a dairy beside, where they cooled and bottled the milk produced from 15 cows, housed in farm buildings halfway down nearby Castle Street. Sidney would then go out with a small cart and sell the milk to all the people of the village. All the meadows for the cows were around a Norman and Roman Castle built on the seashore facing Portsmouth Harbour. I looked forward to visiting them there in the future.

At last it was time for us to move on. Letters to Uncle William in London had resulted in confirmation of their invitation to stay with them. We said all our goodbyes and boarded a train in Portsmouth to Waterloo station in London. Here we took a bus to their house in north London, where he had moved to since he had retired from his work with the Cadbury Pratt Company in central London.

London was as busy as ever, I was somehow glad that we were now in the city, the hustle and bustle, bright lights and traffic, red buses and black taxis, huge shops and restaurants.

Auntie Mabel welcomed us with open arms. The new house was large so there was plenty of room for us, our bedroom was large and we had a bathroom to ourselves. Glory be, what heaven! It was nice to be able to go outside and catch a bus wherever we wanted to go. During the next few days we recounted again our saga of father's disgrace and subsequent death. Saying that it was our intention to make England our home and that we would find some accommodation and I would look for work. London would be a good place to start.

During the next few weeks we scoured the city and eventually found a small flat at the top of a large Victorian house, called Maitland Park House, Maitland Park Road, off Haverstock Hill, N.W.3.

The next problem was to find work. Uncle William was a treasure in helping me he gave me introductions to every person who he thought might help me. I must have had interviews with at least ten people. Armed with my references I was more than confident I would find something satisfactory.

It was now December and it looked as though we would be here for Christmas. Auntie Mabel said this would be alright, but she had invited her husbands two Children and their families, so that the house would be full up. Mother volunteered to help with the cleaning and cooking. Auntie Mabel was delighted. We all looked forward to the festive celebrations.

It was one day during November when I was looking for work that my path took me through central London, seeing the Canadian flag flying outside a very imposing building I went to investigate and found it was the Canadian Embassy that I had been to before, I decided to go inside to inquire about my friend Morveth who I had met on my previous visit to England.

Sure enough she was still working there. We had lunch together and arranged a meeting at the following weekend. Again I had a lot to tell her, she said that since we had last met she had lost her parents and was living alone in their house on the outskirts of the city. Our friendship grew quickly and from there on we saw each other regularly, usually shopping and afterwards having afternoon tea at Fortnum and Masons, Uncle William's old company. During our conversations she thought I should apply for a British passport as I intended to live in the U.K. She said that it would not affect my current Canadian passport which I could still keep as I was born in Canada. As I had two British parents I was entitled to a British one. This I did and to the end of my life I kept two passports.

One day during our weekend meetings Morveth said would I like to become involved in a pilgrimage to Vimy Ridge in France. The Canadian Government had erected a huge modern memorial monument to commemorate the Canadian troops killed in that great battle during the last war. Many Canadians were coming to the U.K. to attend the ceremony and were staying in London. A special pilgrimage was arranged for them. Special ferries across the English Channel had been booked as they were expecting several thousand people. The new King would be there to lay the first wreath followed by the all the leaders of the Canadian Government. I thought I could not refuse as this was my heritage. Morveth said she would include me as her friend on the list of pilgrims from the Embassy. Two days after the ceremony the king would invite all the pilgrims to a tea party in the grounds of Buckingham Palace. We both could go if we wished. All this was planned to take place next year during July 1936. I awaited this event with great pride.

During the rest of November and December I was out and about looking for employment. I must have had at least ten interviews, some I disliked immensely and did not follow them up. Then at breakfast one morning Uncle William said he had seen a friend of his who was looking for a head clerk to replace an old employee who was retiring. If I was interested I should arrange an appointment that I did without delay.

On the appointed day, armed with all my references I confidently entered the office of Mr Sloan, Clerk and Superintendent to the Corporation of London, Spitalfields Market, E.1. He was in charge of the main market, the Flower Market and the London Fruit Exchange. He was a delightful man who made me feel at ease at once. The interview lasted about one hour and I felt I had made a good impression. He was particularly interested in my references about which he questioned me at length. However, he said he could not make a decision that day as he had more applicants to see. He would write to me as soon as he had made a decision. I awaited that letter with hope and impatience.

At length it came to say I was required for a second interview. This was good news indeed. The second meeting was very different from the first, he went into greater depth and escorted me around the Markets where I would be working. At the end of the morning he sat me down and said that I had secured the post. I was so thankful. We now had a home in this great city and an income that would enable us to live quite well providing we were not too lavish.

The bus stop, nearly outside our flat, was most convenient. It was only a short bus ride down the City Road to Liverpool St Station where the Market was nearby. Mr Sloan asked me to start after the Christmas break. Mother and I were pleased about everything that had happened so quickly. Everything seemed to be going our way. On Sunday we went to Christ Church, Spitalfields, to thank God for our good fortune. My diary records my feelings and relief that we had arrived at this point in our life.

Christmas 1935 was enjoyed by all the family at Aunty Mabel's and we were no exception. In our new home we celebrated the New Year 1936 with a bottle of sherry. Mother was busy looking for good second-hand furniture to make our flat a home.

The first Monday in the New Year 1936, I started work at Spitalfields. My office was next to Mr Sloans with a good view over the busy street below. The rest of the staff in the office were somewhat suspicious of the new face as head clerk. Especially as I had a Canadian accent, which most people thought was American. After about four weeks we began to get on better together and I thought I was gaining their confidence. The work was interesting and enjoyable, particularly when I had to go down to the flower market where the scent was almost overpowering.

Things in London seemed to be going on so quickly that I could hardly keep pace with it. On January 22nd 1936 the Accession of the new King Edward V111 was announced with great pomp from the steps of all the major government buildings in London. This was of course well reported in the press together with their opinions about his relationship with the American lady Mrs Simpson.

My new job took up most of my time, learning about the Market routines and finding out who was in charge of what. I put in a lot of extra hours during the evenings to satisfy myself that I was aware of the most important aspects of the office management.

Weekends were mostly taken up with shopping for Mother and helping her about the flat. As usual I sat down and wrote to Mary and Margaret Matheson, and Nora Moorhead, my good friend and competitor at Havergal College, Winnipeg, telling them about our making a home in London and about my new job.

1936 went by very quickly and by June I was able to spend more time with Morveth exploring more of central London, particularly inside the ring of City Walls where most of the Historical buildings were located. One weekend Mother and I decided to go up to Nottingham to see Fathers relatives. We stayed with Archie at his house together with Joyce his wife and Sylvia. We told them about our problems in Canada and our decision to return to England for good. We also met Auntie Daisy and her son Phillip, who was about my age. I thought he was very good looking, he certainly had a very nice disposition and we found we had a lot in common. The weekend slipped by quickly and we had to return home promising to visit them again soon. We now had seen all our relatives in England. They all now knew why we had planned our future in the U.K. So we made our way home and settled down to our life in London.

At the end of July came the dedication of the Canadian War Memorial in France. I explained to Mr Sloan what had happened and the invitation to accompany Morveth for the ceremony. I said I would not take any holidays to compensate for my two days I would be away from work. He agreed and said they would manage somehow.

On the 26th July we found ourselves at Dover ready to go aboard the ferry to Calais. Once in France we were met by a fleet of buses that took us all the way to Vimy.

The ceremony was due to start at 3.00 p.m. Hundreds of Canadian soldiers were there together with their wonderful Military Bands. The Highland regiments were very smart in their kilts. All the Canadian Government Officials were there together with The King and his military entourage. The service was conducted by the Archbishop of Ottawa. It was a moving service. It was very sad to see the relatives of the fallen weeping to see their sons name on the stonework. I was never more proud to be a Canadian. We could not stay long as we had to get back to Calais for the ferry by 9.00p.m. We slept on the ferry overnight and arrived back in London at midday. Two days later we went to the reception of the Royal Garden Party at Buckingham Palace. This was wonderful as I met many fellow Canadians and was able get a good view of the new King.

Back to work again but found time to rush down to Horse Guards Parade to see the trooping of the colours, again a wonderful ceremony. By this time all the newspapers were full of the Governments attitude to the Kings relationship with Mrs Simpson. They would not allow an American to be Queen. It was unconstitutional. I thought the King would be a very good Monarch as he was always championing workingmen, trying to get better conditions.

Arrangements were in hand for the new Kings Coronation due later in the year. But due to the Royal Families domestic problem everything was put on hold pending clarification of his personal position.

During the early part of December, King Edward VIII made a radio broadcast to the nation and to the British Empire saying that he was not prepared to carry out his duties as King without the woman he loved. Therefore he wished to abdicate his present position forthwith. Glory be! Was this man mad or was he trying to tell the public that he could not perform the duties of King without a wife who loved him irrespective of what nationality she was?

I wondered what would happen next. But I think everybody was expecting this and an announcement was made saying that his brother George would be proclaimed King the following day. Sure enough at 11a.m a proclamation was made to the effect that as from this hour Albert Frederick Arthur George and his wife Elizabeth would be crowned King George VI and Queen Elizabeth at a coronation to be arranged later.

I was overjoyed that they already had two daughters. It would make a good Royal Family. As usual I sat down and wrote a letter to Buckingham Palace saying how thrilled I was in spite of their difficulties to have them as my Royal Family. I wished them luck and a happy future.

So ended my first year in England. The future looked bright for us.

CHAPTER SEVEN

Mother and I now settled down to our new life. Our top floor flat was warm and comfortable and we had been able to furnish it satisfactory. Mrs Chalk, the owner of the property, treated us as if we were part of her family, asking us down for tea and during the summer we had drinks in her delightful garden that we could use at any time. Mother was making a lot of friends with the local Mothers Union which brought her some more work, dressmaking and alterations. As for me, I was enjoying my work and thankful that our financial situation was improving by the month. London captivated me, I could not see enough of the City and enjoyed the ambience. Morveth was a regular theatregoer and asked me to accompany her to many of the major shows in the West End. We joined the throngs waiting to see the Stars. We would finish our day out in town with an afternoon tea at Fortnum & Masons, "don't tell me exclaimed Morveth it's Uncle William's old firm." These were memorable occasions.

I began to realise that I was happier in the City environment than out in the country where my closest relatives lived. I was not happy to sit at home during the long winter nights but preferred to be out visiting friends or inviting them to our home. My love of letter writing continued to occupy some of my spare time, I wrote to Buckingham Palace, expressing my hopes that the new King and Queen and their family would be happy in their new circumstances and that as a Canadian I was sure that most of my fellow countrymen wished them well. Letters also went back to all my friends in Canada, especially to Margaret and Mary Matheson and their Mother and Father,

Most Sundays we would attend Church at Christ Church, Spitalfields and therefore made many friends among the congregation. Our lives were as good as we could hope and during the rest of the year continued in the same pattern.

Christmas came and went and we celebrated New Years Day 1938 with Morveth and friends with a party at her house. Auntie Mabel and Uncle William also asked us round for drinks and were pleased to hear we were so happy.

Sometime during April I was surprised to get an official looking letter from the Lord Chamberlains Office. It was an invitation by Their Majesties to an Afternoon Party in the Garden of Buckingham Palace on Thursday 21st July 1938. From 4 to 6.30 p.m. [weather permitting] Morning Dress. My goodness! Glory be! What a surprise, what had I done to deserve this? I looked forward to this event with relish. When it came the afternoon was fine and dry. I took a taxi to the Palace and clutching my invitation entered at the appropriate gate. The gateman checked me off on the guest list and I was allowed to go through. A Military Band was playing all the popular tunes. I mixed with all the other people from all over the world and at last caught sight of the Royal Couple, casually walking among the guests, chatting to many people. I thoroughly enjoyed the afternoon and came away thankful that I had written my letters to the Royal Family.

All the year I was engrossed in my work and did not take any annual holidays. Mr Sloan was pleased with my dedication to work and our relationship grew enormously, so much so that at the end of the year he said that I should take some time off. The Market was undergoing major alterations and it would be a good time to catch up on the accrued holiday entitlement. I was luke-warm about this suggestion and said I would think about it.

It was coincidence that the next day I received a reply from my letter to Margaret Matheson, giving me all her news and surprise, surprise, an invitation to her wedding, to be held in the St Johns Cathedral. Winnipeg. The service conducted by her Father, the Bishop.

In the office the next day I showed this letter to Mr Sloan, who said I should think about going. I said it would be too long away from work as it would take me at least three weeks to make the journey, see all my friends and attend the wedding. No problem, he said, he would ask the previous person who did my job, and was now retired, to come in and cover me for the time I was away.

What should I do? That evening I told Mother what had happened, she thought for a moment and then said that I should go alone. She would be quite happy on her own for a few weeks and it would be nice for me to see all my old friends. The next day I asked Mr Sloan if he was serious about my taking time off, I had a guilty conscience about going but he said it would be perfectly alright it would not affect my job.

Mother was happy and so was Mr Sloan. I would go back to Canada for the wedding. The next day I went to the travel agents and arranged a passage at the appropriate time to coincide with the wedding. This time, however, as it was winter I would have to go via New York. Letters went off to Margaret and Mrs Matheson expressing my delight at the invitation and my acceptance.

On 3rd December I was at Liverpool and boarded the Liner, which I think was the S.S. LAURENTIC, bound for New York. The journey took 6 days, after which I took the train for Toronto. This was the original route that Mother and Father took when they first came to Canada. I had of course written to all my friends that I was coming to Canada for Margaret's Wedding but by this time some of them had moved from Winnipeg to other places where they had obtained work. I did not stay in Toronto but continued my journey to Winnipeg at once. It was not until the 10th December that I finally arrived in the City.

My first call was to Mrs Matheson who received me with open arms and wanted to know all our news. I brought a long letter from Mother for her, which told of our movements since leaving Winnipeg and thanking her for all her kind help in the past. I stayed at their house until the wedding, which was very special for me as I was able to meet many old friends from my schooldays. I went unannounced to the Hydro Company and there saw all my old office friends, including Mr Glassco, Mr Sawyer and Mr Andrews. We had a very happy time together that afternoon and they asked me when I was going to return. I said that I had now made my home in England I had no plans to return.

It was there that I again made contact with the League of Tramps and they invited me to accompany them on a Christmas tour. I readily accepted providing that I could be back in time to catch my Liner back to England on the 22nd December. They took me to Montreal, Niagara Falls, and then on the long train journey to Vancouver. In the party were my old friends Veronica, Emily Hay, Margaret Effie and Ruth; we visited the grave of Captain George Vancouver, the founder of the City.

I was obliged to leave the party in Vancouver as time was running out and travelled back to Winnipeg. Bishop Matheson talked to me about our experiences and gave me confidence for the future. On the next Sunday at the Cathedral he gave me communion. I was pleased to be back in Canada and enjoying the break, but something told me my future lay in Europe. I was pleased to be going home. Christmas was spent on board the Liner to Liverpool. It was a very lively occasion that passed the time as very few people could go on deck during the winter storms. Mother had spent her Christmas with Auntie Mabel and Uncle William.

It was with great pleasure that we were together again in our little flat and I returned to work after Christmas.

1939 arrived with much speculation about the probability of a war with Germany. Every newspaper carried articles about the Munich agreement with Hitler and the part occupation of Czechoslovakia, Much activity was going on in London, plans were being drawn up to protect the population during likely air attacks. Bomb shelters were being built in the parks and in every street. Air raid wardens were recruited to advise the people what to do. Gas masks were issued to everyone and it was an offence to travel without them.

Mother, Mrs Chalk and I talked about the situation every night but as usual, we just hoped it wouldn't happen and it would go away. Everyone at work was worried about the future, most of the young men in the market of military age were called up for service in the armed forces. The whole Country was rearming and the City was busier that ever.

Easter came along, and I decided to visit my relatives down in Hampshire. I travelled by train to Portsmouth and then by bus to Portchester, about 7 miles outside the City where cousin Rose and Sidney were now living in a new house in Castle St., only a short walk from the old Roman Castle Ruins which ran down to the shore and looked out over the harbour to the City and Naval Base of Portsmouth about two miles away. There I met their family and stayed for three days visiting Auntie Ginny and Uncle Bill and cousin Tinnie and Fred and their two children.

[Author note : during this stay with our family I really got to know Mabel well. She was elegant and soft spoken with that fascinating Canadian accent, She was as clever as she was beautiful. She was 32 years old. Her tales of her travels kept my imagination working overtime and I wondered whether I would ever be able to see the places she had seen. I was ten years old at the time and this was the first time I had met anyone from overseas].

I returned to work after Easter and the implementation of the new war regulations made my work more difficult. Shortage of trained staff necessitated me working late to keep abreast of the accounts. The weeks went by with more scares of imminent war, There was no way in which I would be able to take a holiday with the work on hand.

One day the postman brought a similar letter to the one that I had received from the Lord Chamberlains Office. It was an invitation to another Garden Party at Buckingham Palace but this time it was for Mother. It was to be held on Thursday, 20th July. Mother was overjoyed and readily accepted, I can only suppose that when I had attended the last one I had spoken to several people that I was living with my widowed Mother who would have liked to come but was not invited. However, whatever the reason mother enjoyed it and talked about it for days afterwards.

A few days latter Mother received a letter from cousin Nellie saying that she would be expecting her second child in early September, Mother decided she ought to go and help out. Therefore on Sunday 3rd September, the very day that war was declared on Germany, she went down to Stanford Cottage, South Warnborough in Hampshire to look after the household. She stayed until after the event on 6th September and ran the house with her usual efficiency, she returned to London on the 20th September just in time to witness the first Air Raid over London. Barrage balloons were flying all over London to prevent bombers from flying low. Anti aircraft guns were situated in all the parks and open spaces. However on this occasion we did not see any German planes and the All Clear siren went after about three hours.

Now that the war had started everything began to happen. All vehicles had their lights masked and no shops or houses were allowed to show any lights outside their buildings. Mother and Mrs Chalk made special thick black curtains to hang at the windows that did not show any light outside. We also decided to transform the cellar into a bedroom where we could all sleep as this was, we were told, the only safe place in any house if we had a bomb explode nearby. We moved our spare beds down there and made it as comfortable as possible. We would only use them when there was a raid.

We were surprised that nothing happened in London for weeks on end. Our army was stationed all along the Belgian border where as far as we knew no fighting was taking place. It was a period that became known as The Phoney War. Food rationing was introduced and we could not get any fruit or food that had to be imported. We adjusted our cooking accordingly. Christmas was celebrated with the usual decorations and in spite of the food shortages we just made do.

The new year of 1940 brought a complete turnaround in our fortunes.

During the spring the German Army invaded Belgium and the British Army moved forward to meet the enemy. We were sad that they could not stop their advance, our army was not strong enough nor was the Belgian army. In the south the Germans advanced through the Ardennes and Luxembourg and crossed the border into France. The retreat continued all along the front and before long the Belgian army collapsed leaving the British army to defend northern France. The French army tried to stem the advance in the south but again they were unsuccessful. The Germans were now moving swiftly into France, aiming for Paris. The British army was pushed back into a small area around Dunkirk.

We, in London watched this dreadful retreat splashed all across the newspapers and every hour on the radio. What would happen? Everyone at work and in the streets was certain that if this retreat continued we in England would be invaded next. The Prime Minister, Mr Chamberlain assured us that everything was being done to defend our country but he decided that perhaps someone else would be able to lead the country better than him and therefore resigned.

On the 10th May Mr Winston Churchill was appointed Prime Minister. We hoped he would be made of sterner stuff than his predecessor. We need not have worried, he at once ordered the Royal Navy to evacuate all British troops from France across the English Channel. Every boat, Royal Navy or private, capable of crossing the water went to their aid and by the end of the month most of our troops were rescued including many Frenchmen.

By the middle of June the Germans were in control of all the Atlantic coast of France. This meant of course that we could expect an invasion at any time. I wrote to all my relatives on the south coast asking what their plans were if such an invasion happened. The south coast was now in the front line and a no-go area was declared which meant that no one could enter the restricted area. Their letters back to me all said that they would stay where they were and accept the consequences. All men just over military age were advised to volunteer for a Home Guard and within two weeks a million men had signed up all over the country. Sidney was one of the many to volunteer at Portchester. The Government then decided that all children under 10 years old should be moved out of the cities and other areas likely to be attacked by bombers. This meant of course that Roses children could be evacuated. It was not compulsory but anyone with relations or contacts in the country should consider sending their children there for safety.

The Government decided that they would arrange for boatloads of children to be sent to Canada for safety for the duration of the war. One boat of children had already gone and they were planning a second. I wrote to Rosie, suggesting that perhaps I could arrange for her son, Kenneth, to go to some of my friends in Toronto. I was sure he would be happy there and certainly very safe. Rosie wrote back to say that she and Sidney reluctantly agreed to my proposal and gave me permission to proceed if it was possible. I sent a cable to my friend Mary Muir at 27 Braemar Avenue, Toronto, Ontario, explaining the circumstances.

On the 2nd July we received a reply by cable.

"Received your cable. Am considering your proposal. Letter to follow. Mary M"

On the 10th July we received the following letter.

Dear Mabel.

Received your cable or your dear Mothers, don't know which. I cabled back the only short message I felt I could send. My husband and I talked it over and feel if Kenneth would be happy with us we could easily have him to stay here as we have an extra bedroom. But, if we found he needed the companionship of another boy we know several people who would be pleased to take him, I feel sure. We have a very fine school one block from our home, so altogether we are very conveniently situated. Also two blocks from Upper Canada College { Private school for boys}. We do like our duplex so much and are very happy in it and so peaceful.

When we read of the terrific air raids over there, we do feel fortunate. Do hope and pray for your safety, also Mothers.

My love to you both and regards

Affectionately

Mary Muir

Cousin Rosie wrote off to the Evacuation Authorities asking if her son could be included in the scheme, as friends had offered to give him a home in Toronto for the duration of the war. The reply was immediate, he could be included. He was to report to the evacuation office at Liverpool Docks on the 15th August together with his clothes, in a small suitcase, and his credentials.

Mother and I were pleased that we had been able to help. And looked forward to hearing about the trip and Kenneth's reactions to his new home. We knew that this would be very traumatic for him.

Life in the East End of London continued as hectic as usual. At work we employed more women to replace the men but the market was suffering because of the limited importation of luxury fruit and flowers. I had taken to the habit of walking to work each day and therefore was able to talk to people on my way. I never ceased to be amazed at the confidence and spirit of the locals. They were sure that Hitler would not drive them from their homes, and would fight him if he tried.

Tragedy struck a few days later. A Liner taking children to Canada was torpedoed and sunk off the southwest coast of Ireland, in spite of displaying Red Crosses on her sides. Only a few of the 600 children on board were saved.

This was Headlines the next day in the newspapers and on the radio. How merciless could the Germans be? This news was of course, received by Rose and Sidney with terrible shock. Their own son would be going the same route soon. The next day Sidney cancelled Kenneth's passage, saying that if he was to die he would die with all of them at home. Rose wrote to Mary Muir and explained.

On the 10th November Mary wrote to Rose as follows:-

Dear Mrs Parrett.

Have been intending to write to you for some time to thank you for the snap of Kenneth also your kind letter. We were dreadfully disappointed that he did not arrive, but we can understand your concern about the risks he would be taking at sea. We were so looked forward to having him with us this winter, in fact we had his room all ready for him. What trying days you are all having. My thoughts are with you all constantly. Good luck and good health to you all from

Mary and Bill.

I sent a letter dated 16th July 1940 to Rose in Hampshire as follows:-

My dear Rose.

Thanks so much for your letter received this morning. We were delighted to hear from you and to hear the news that you are all O.K. What times you are having! If you would like a rest why don't you come up to stay with us for a while and bring Marianne too [Roses third child] *. Next week all being well, I am going down to Ogmore-by-Sea. Near Bridged, South Wales to stay with Esther before it is a prohibited area. I have managed a weeks holiday, so am looking forward to it very much. So do come, it would be a rest for you. Our days and nights are entirely peaceful, no excitement at all.*

I do wish it were not so exciting down your way. How are Uncle and Auntie at Boar hunt standing up to it. I'll bet Tinnie is all of a dither now. But if we can only stick it out, I am certain we shall win in the long run. I see the Axis has its eye on London next, so I suppose our turn will come. Did you hear the account on Sunday night by Charles Gardiner on the BBC {On an air battle} You would have thought it was an exciting international ice hockey game, instead of a life and death struggle .

Funnily enough, by the same mail this morning there came a letter from Mary Muir. Offering to take Ken. You see it is Mary who is offering to take him so when you write address it to Mrs Muir. Mrs Payne is Mary's mother who lives with them. Mary married a widower, some years older that herself. Bill had a boy Keith who is now grown up and in the Air Force at Winnipeg. Mary and Bill have no children. They are a nice couple and I know would care for Ken like their own son. He would have a lovely home and Mrs Payne is a darling- she is Mothers friend and would be kindness itself to Ken.

What a pity they have stopped the evacuation scheme but I am sure it will begin again. I suppose you have made the necessary enquiries and filled in the forms as when it starts Ken should certainly get one of the first opportunities, considering he is in such a vulnerable area. I take it they are not evacuating his school. By the way, about his education if he goes to Toronto, I presume he will go to the school Mary mention.[not Upper Canada College, which is dreadfully expensive]. You needn't worry about his education for I know Toronto schools have a very high standard. Do let me know what happens about it all.

The Beaver Club [in London, where I help out in the evenings] is very busy at the moment, throngs of Canadian soldiers go through there. I expect I shall do some more nights when I come back from my Holiday. Yes it is too bad we cannot come down to see you for a while as yours is a prohibited area. But you must come up instead. I am very disappointed, as I had hoped to hop down for a week, Raids or no.

Did Auntie Ginny get her wool. The wine flecked grey, it is impossible to get it up here. I tried a good many shops with no luck. You see, on account of the war they are not doing mixtures.

I wonder if Nellie is having raids too. Well the weather seems to have changed but I suppose it is to our benefit. The sooner this Island is shrouded in rain and fog, the better. Anyhow, Keep smiling and keep up your high spirits, that's the spirit that wins wars. How is Sidney, Does he have lots of duty with the Home Guard?

Affectionately as ever.

Mabel.

(Author Note: You will notice from the above correspondence that the South Coast of England was being targeted by the German Air Force - Military installations, Docks, Harbours, Factories, Airfields or anything likely to be of assistance to the defence of the U.K.).

Mother and I were watching the news every day to see where they struck the previous day. We were so worried about all our relations in Hampshire; Portsmouth and Southampton were key targets.

So began the Battle of Britain. Each day on my way to work and returning home in the evenings we saw lots of British fighter planes flying high over London towards the south coast. The county of Kent and Sussex saw most of the action. My heart went out to those young men, sometimes no older that 20; flying perhaps to their death. Each night on the BBC news reports we heard the progress of the battles. Our losses were high but the enemy lost a lot more. Occasionally battles were fought over London where we were able to watch in fear and trepidation. High up, the fighter planes turned and twisted, their contrails forming patterns in the sky, sometimes a plane would fall in flames, was it ours?

The terrific air battles continued right through July, August and into September when suddenly they stopped, The Government claimed that a victory had been achieved, the German air force lost so many planes they could not continue.

When I came back from my few days in South Wales, I went to the Beaver Club to offer my services on a more regular basis in the evenings and weekends. The Beaver Club was catering for Canadian servicemen in London on leave from all three services. There I met many Airmen who had been fighting in the Battle of Britain. I never ceased to admire their courage, one moment they were in the air in danger of their lives and the next back on their base in the bars drinking as if nothing had happened. Sometimes they would fly three missions a day. After the Dunkirk evacuation we received many army men who told me of their experiences. I admired them all, and grieved for their fallen comrades.

The air battle over the south coast may have nearly stopped but the Germans thought that perhaps if they bombed London by night to avoid the fighters the English would surrender. On the 7th September in the evening, about 9.p.m., the sirens sounded a warning, I was at home that night, and being September it was still light. We went outside to see if we could see anything, but nothing was happening. At about 10 p.m. we heard the drone of aircraft, a constant throbbing. A sound we had not heard before. The guns began to fire and when dark enough the searchlights scanned the sky. The noise was constant. Later we heard loud explosions which we were told were bombs in the docks, not very far away. We retreated very quickly to our cellar to await developments. The explosions continued for a very long time and the guns never stopped firing. We were both terrified. This was the first time we had been under attack. I am not ashamed to say we never prayed for our safety more earnestly than that night.

At about 3.a.m. things began to die down and eventually the All Clear siren sounded. Fire engines were rushing around with their sirens sounding, so we knew there were problems in the docks. The next day I took a bus to work. It was diverted down new roads as the normal ones were blocked, but eventually I got to work. The devastation was terrible, whole terraces of houses were demolished. And rescue men were still working to bring out the injured and dead. I just sat in my office and looked out of the window where I could still see men working to clear the streets. I just cried when I saw weeping mothers calling for their children under the debris.

The next weekend Mother and I helped out with the evacuation of the local children to the countryside. The Red Cross, St Johns, W.V.S. Police and other social workers together with Teachers and Parents all gathered at the schools where each child was given a label with their name and address and next of kin details. This was pinned to their collars, and together with their gas masks and small cases they assembled in the playground.

Every class was escorted by their teachers and parents along the streets and pavements to the local railway station. It was pitiful to hear the sobs and wailing of the children who were leaving their parents for the first time and going of to somewhere they knew not where. At the station a carriage was allocated to each class. When the children were all aboard the Parents said goodbye. All of them cried and hugged their children, wiped running noses and kissed them a hundred times, saying, please write home as soon as you can. I was glad I was not a parent. Many of these children went to homes that were large and beautifully furnished with large gardens, completely different from that which they were accustomed in the East End. Many had not even seen a field or a copse, let alone horses, cows, sheep and pigs. The new environment was unsettling for some and many returned home in a short while. Some, however made new friends and were perfectly happy.

The raids continued with increased velocity, covering the whole of London. The East End was worst hit. Our house suffered two near misses, causing the roof to be blown off. There were not many nights that we were not visited by the Germans. Thousands of houses were demolished and hundreds killed and wounded. Each night at about 9.p.m. they would arrive, bedlam was unleashed and we retired to our cellar for safety. Only those who were there can possibly imagine the noise, smell of burning houses and cries of the wounded. Firemen, Rescuers, medical teams and Policemen all working together. Buses and cars thrown upside down by the bomb blasts. Holes in the roads. All supplies of gas, electricity and water were cut off.

Mobile canteens, run by the W.V.S. and The Salvation Army supplied a constant supply of tea and sandwiches to the homeless. Religious personnel from all the denominations went about their business giving comfort and blessings to the bereaved.

The Blitz continued all through the year. All the major cities of the U.K. were bombed including Belfast in Northern Ireland. I considered if we had done the right thing to have moved from the safe haven of Canada. But Mother was determined to see it through. She was however terrified of the bombing and could not bear to be left alone all day. She therefore spent most of her time with Mrs Chalk downstairs. As time went by I could see she was not eating as she should and was losing weight. Every time the sirens sounded she would retire to the cellar to just sit and shake. This continued and we discussed what should be done, if anything.

Fate however decided for us. Early October brought one of the heaviest raids yet. I thought Mother would go mad. A bomb fell about 50 yards away from our house and the blast blew the roof off, we had no electricity or water. We lived with Mrs Chalk in the cellar for about a week when Mother said this was enough and we should move out of London as soon as possible. I reluctantly agreed and the next day tendered my resignation to Mr Sloan, he said he was sorry to see me go as we had such a good relationship, but the market was getting more difficult to run and maybe would close for the duration of the war. When I got home that night Mother had sold all our furniture to a dealer. Mr Sloan very kindly gave me a reference, which he thought would be useful in the future:-

Corporation of London.

Spitalfields Market.

London.E.1.

5th October 1940.

To whom it may concern.

I have pleasure in stating that Miss Mabel Pyniger served on the permanent staff of this department from the 5th December 1937 until 5th October 1940 as a senior stenographer and that she resigned her position of her own accord as she is leaving London for family reasons.

During her service here, in addition to performing the more important typewriting and stencilling, she also took charge of all filing and carried out much work of a secretarial nature, and in every thing she undertook she showed marked ability and a sound knowledge of office organisation.

Miss Pynigar has a pleasant manner and is tactful. She was punctual and regular in her attendance at the office and I can with confidence recommend her for any position requiring organising or administrative ability.

Yours faithfully,

J.E.Sloan.

Clerk and Superintendent.

The following day we ordered a taxi and drove down to North Hampshire to cousin Nellie's house at South Warnborough where we arrived unannounced late at night. They had no phone so that we could not tell them we were coming. Nellie and husband John were very concerned at this sudden intrusion into their family. However after some explanation we were accepted and made welcome. Except for the taxi driver who was very irate because a jar of honey had leaked out all over his jacket!

We stayed with Nellie for some weeks, helping her with the household chores and paying for our board and lodgings. Mother was pleased to be away from the bombing and began to eat again, however I was out of a job and it was imperative that I found employment as soon as possible and of course somewhere to live, which was safe from the bombers. During this time I spent most of my time writing to most of my friends telling what we had done and where we were staying. Among those to whom I wrote was a letter to Mothers good friend Mrs Twining who lived in Oxford, and had always kept in touch. She wrote back at once saying we could go up to Oxford and stay with her while I perhaps looked for work.

This was on opportunity I could not miss and it was arranged that we should go at once. Mother was pleased to see her old friend again and while I went to search for work. Mother brought her up to date with our problems. My first call was to the employment exchange where a very helpful lady went through all the vacancies in Oxford. Of those that I thought suitable was one at the Town Hall. They required a secretary who would be prepared to do other tasks as and when they arose. The employment exchange made an appointment for me and I went along at the appointed time clutching all my references. The interview was by the Town Clerk, Mr Harry Plowman. He was most impressed with my record and quite understood why I had decided to leave London. My luck was in. He agreed to employ me and asked if I could start at once. I said that I was temporarily staying with friends but now that I had obtained employment I would be looking for accommodation in Oxford. He advised me to go to the housing department who he thought could help me. As soon as I left him I went there and found that Mr Plowman had telephoned them to ask their assistance in finding me accommodation. They recommended a flat available at 77 Windmill Road, Headington, East Oxford.

I returned home to Mother with the good news. She was "over the moon" and we decided to go to inspect it the following day. 77 Windmill Rd was a red brick house of fairly modern design. The top flat was spacious and clean. We agreed to take it at once.

We never went back to Nellie's house but moved in straight away. I also started work at the Town Hall the following Monday. The flat was partially furnished so that we could manage quite well. Mrs Twining, Mothers friend who lived nearby had a large house, gave us bits of furniture to fill the gaps as she had too much. She had three daughters Margaret, Gwyneth and Betty, to whom I became quite friendly as time passed.

My work at the Town Hall was much the same as I had been doing in London, but I am afraid the systems were very much outdated. I was given the task of updating the whole office; this modernising aspect I enjoyed very much. Taking minutes of the various meetings was very interesting. This of course was what I had been trained for in Canada. During my five and a half years that I stayed with the Council I worked with six Mayors.

Having established ourselves in Oxford we set about visiting all the beautiful Colleges and Churches. They say that Oxford is the city of dreaming spires. There certainly were a lot of them. The difference between the East End and here was dramatic, the city was a Major University and every thing seemed to be affiliated to learning. The streets were teeming with scholars and professors, all riding bikes, which was the quickest way to get about down all the alleyways. But since we had been here we had not had one Air Raid. What a relief!

We now settled down to our new surroundings and once again tried to improve our finances. I was very happy in my new job, as I was interested in the different committees that met each week to discuss local problems. I took down all the minutes and distributed them to all concerned. My chief pleasure was to accompany the Mayors on their duties out in the City and to keep them briefed on the subjects in question. In this way I was able to see parts of the City that the tourists were unable to. I met many famous personalities in the Government, Services and Industry. Some I liked and some I did not.

This period of my life was one that I look back on as being the time when I was able to give Mother a home where she could relax and make friends, with no problems associated with the war. Mrs Twining introduced her to many neighbours and accompanied her to the local Church where she joined the Mothers Union and made many new friends; we both attended Church most Sundays. It was good to see Mother in fairly good health for a woman of 67 years. She had been moving around all her life, caused by her matrimonial problems. Here was a place where she had time to reflect on the past and talk about our future. She often wondered why I had not met any young man with whom I could develop a relationship. Here I was, nearly 35 years old with no prospects in that direction. I have to admit that with the hindsight of Mothers problems it did not give me much enthusiasm to think about marriage. I never discussed the topic if I could help it.

As time went by I was able to visit many friends during my holidays. We were able to go up to Nottingham to see auntie Daisy and her son Phillip. Phillip asked me to accompany him on a trip to Wales that he had planned. As I said before, I liked him very much and agreed to go. We went in his car and toured the northern area, which was very pretty with beautiful mountains and rivers. It was a great laugh, as we could not understand the Welsh language. However, if Mother thought that this would be the start of a relationship, she was mistaken. Phillip and I remained good friends only.

The years slipped by and it was not long before the end of the war in Europe was in sight. The Germans surrendered to the Allies and Mr Churchill called for a day of celebration and thanksgiving which was to be on 8th May 1945. Victory in Europe day was celebrated all over the country with street parties and dancing. We were so pleased that we had escaped to Oxford and had established ourselves in the community.

My work at the Council Offices continued to be absorbing my interests and keeping me very busy. As the war was over I was able to take my holidays at the usual times and my weekends were always free. I started to visit all my friends and relatives, especially those in Hampshire that I had been unable to see due to the restrictions.

One friend that I visited was Dorothy who I had met while I was in London during my many shopping expeditions. She modelled shoes for Raynes Shoe shops and we became very good friends. Dorothy eventually retired and made her home in Bournemouth where I visited her whenever I was in that area.

During the summer of 1946 I was visiting friends in Oxford when the conversation turned to discussing the positions that women graduates were getting in politics, industry and in the civil service. The University had created a special department called the OXFORD UNIVERSITY WOMENS APPOINTMENTS COMMITTEE at No 41, St Giles, in the City. I thought that this sounded very interesting and made inquiries if there were any positions available in that office. One of my favourite sayings was that there was "nothing for the dumb" I therefore went there to inquire about employment. The secretary, Miss D. Fone, very kindly agreed to see me and after a lengthy conversation and looking at my references said that she would give my application further thought. About two weeks later I received a letter to say would I go for a second interview. This time I saw two senior professors who grilled me about my qualification and background. At the end they offered me a position as Assistant Secretary. I therefore gave the Council a month notice. They very kindly gave me a reference.

TOWNHALL OXFORD.

14th August 1946.

To whom it may concern.

Miss M. R. Pyniger entered my department to take up a war- time post and stayed for five and a half years to become on of the most valued members of the staff. She has just left to take up a post elsewhere which is likely to give greater scope for the abilities which she undoubtedly possesses.

Primarily Miss Pyniger was responsible for the whole of the filing work arising from a busy department concerned with complicated and often inter-locking matters, under her supervision the system was completely reorganised and its efficiency materially improved. In addition Miss Pyniger who is a most competent typist, was responsible for fair-copying into the minute books the proceedings of the many committees of the Council, and this work involved the highest degree of neatness and accuracy.

Miss Pyniger has deputised for the Mayors Secretary and undertaken the whole of the work of this post from time to time. This has given her ample opportunity of dealing with people from all walks of life and in attending to the varied requirements of those holding the office of Mayor. In the performance of these tasks she has enjoyed the complete confidence of the various holders of the office.

Miss Pyniger has consistently carried out the responsible duties of her post to my entire satisfaction and I can unreservedly recommend her for any appointment in which the wide experience she has gained in my department and the attributes and qualities which I have mentioned, coupled with those of conscientiousness and a pleasing personality are essential.

Signed.

Harry Plowman.

Town Clerk.

With this glowing reference I started work for the Committee. Apart from normal office work the part I liked best was the times when I was dealing with graduates and undergraduates. They would come into my office and I would listen to their life stories and their hopes for the future when their University days were over. I had to be a good listener and help them decide which direction their career should take according to their degrees and other qualifications. I was a person who enjoyed this situation and felt that I had to pull out all the stops to find what the graduates wanted. We had contacts all over the U.K. and abroad, particularly in the Commonwealth. I was very happy when I was able to find what a graduate wanted and we received many letters of thanks.

While we were very happy in our flat at Windmill Road it was becoming more difficult to maintain. The Flat was spacious and with Mother getting weaker and with my job getting more time consuming we began to look for a smaller flat. We eventually found one at 49 Portland Road, belonging to a Miss Jeans. We moved in as soon as possible. It was only one street away from my friend Betty Twining so that we saw each other quite often.

It was during 1949, during one of my flying visits to cousin Rosie, that I first met Audrey Parrett. Rosie had now moved from Portchester, to get away from the bombing of Portsmouth, and taken a farm in the Meon Valley out in the country. Audrey was engaged to be married to Rose' second son, Ken. I liked her very much and invited them to visit us in Oxford during the summer. They came and spent a week with us. I was able to show them around the City which they enjoyed a lot. Boating on the river with a picnic was the highlight of their stay. Audrey and I became close friends and for many years to come went with her on holidays to Bournemouth and Torquay.

Two and a half years went by and I was more and more involved in the lives of the students, more and more women were getting very responsible jobs, the war had shown them that they could be equal to the men in senior positions. Commonwealth graduates from Africa were a special interest for me, as they were for the first time getting a higher education not available in their own countries. My interest in people gave me much happiness and my circle of friends grew enormously.

Late spring 1949 saw Mothers health deteriorating. Visits to the Doctors resulted in her having to see a Consultant. Her throat had developed a growth that was getting worse. She seemed to get weaker every week in spite of her medication. I found that she was unable to look after herself while I was at work. It was plain that we could not go on with our present arrangements. After much heart searching I decided that it was my duty to be with her full time. It was with great reluctance that the next day I explained the situation to Doris Fone and said that I would like to leave as soon as possible. As the situation was urgent she agreed to let me go at the end of the week, which was very kind.

I went home and did everything I could for Mother during the next few months. I was even able to take her for a little holiday in Bournemouth with Rose. We sat in the Hotel garden looking out to sea towards the Needles on the Isle of Wight, with all the sailing boats with their coloured sails making a glorious picture. This was the last time I was to be on holiday with Mother. On returning home she unfortunately continued to suffer pain and saw the Doctors often. She was admitted to Hospital but there was little they could do, except to ease the pain. She passed away a week later and I arranged a funeral service at the local Church attended by all her friends and by some of my relations from Hampshire including Rose and Sidney. She was buried at Wolvercote Cemetery on 6th June 1949. I bought the plot and made arrangements in my will to be buried in the same grave when my turn came.

Mabel as a baby, with parents John & Rose.

Mabel, aged 6.

Mabel in Brownie uniform.

Rose Pyniger: Mabels mother.

Mabel learning to type.

Boating on the Red River.

Mabel with Margaret and Mary.

Bishop Matheson and wife.

Bishops Court in winter.

The Family at Home: Furby Street.

Graduation Day. Mabel far left.

Father – John Pyniger.

Uncle Bill (Bamp). Game Keeper, Hampshire, UK.

Fathers new car.

R.M.S. Melita. First Liner to England.

On board R.M.S. Melita.

Our house in Furby Street, Winnipeg.

Beardy's Warriors.

Royal Navy Review illuminations.

Royal Yacht Victoria & Albert.

Canadian War Memorial, Vimy, France.

*The Lord Chamberlain is
commanded by Their Majesties to invite*

Miss Mabel R. Pyniger

*to an Afternoon Party in the Garden of Buckingham Palace
on Thursday 21ˢᵗ July 1938, from 4 to 6.30 p.m.
(Weather permitting)*

Morning Dress

| Royal Garden Party Invitations. |

*The Lord Chamberlain is
commanded by Their Majesties to invite*

Mr John Pyniger

*to an Afternoon Party in the Garden of Buckingham Palace,
on Thursday 20ᵗʰ July, 1939, from 4 to 6.30 p.m.
(Weather permitting)*

Morning Dress.

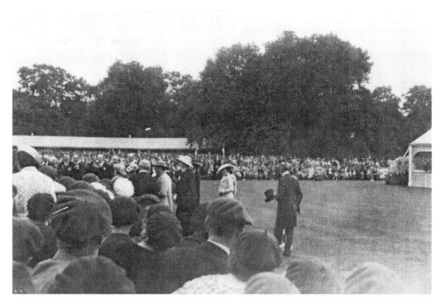

Tea Party: Buckingham Palace, England.

My first child – Nennette in Ghent.

77 Windmill Road, Oxford.

Madam Waks and family in Ghent.

Mr & Mrs Bela – Caux, Switzerland.

Mabel with Kay Kay – Vevey, Switzerland.

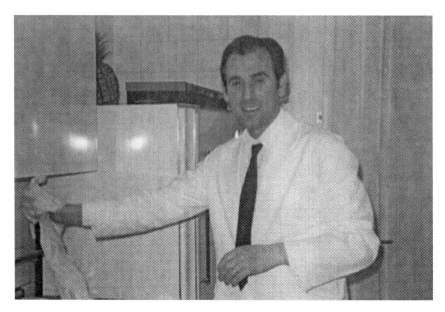

Gino – the Butler.

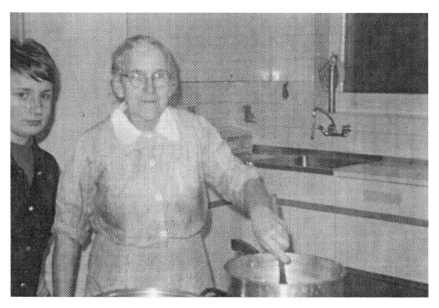

Mary – the Cook.

Yvonne does the shoes!

Ken & Audrey Parrett.

Another Grandchild for Oona.

The Chaplin family 1971.

The Chaplin family 1958.

Victoria – the Ballerina.

Mabel & Ann Hodgeson – Les Avant, Switzerland.

Josphine – the Bride.

Mabel with her friend, Helen.

On holiday – Ireland.

On holiday – Barbados.

On holiday – Eastbourne, England.

Christmas at the Manoir.

Grandma Ya Ya – Greece.

Janes birthday Party.

Going skiing ta Crans Montana.

Lunch at "High Hopes", Barbados.

Wedding in Geneva - Maria & Jonnie Sistovaris.

Mabels birthday – December 1966.

Toronto with friends!

League of Friends – Canada.

Nicky Sistovaris with young Charlie.

Betty Tetrich and Aunty Gypsy.

Young Charlie Sistovaris.

Sir Charles and family at the Manoir.

Mabel with friends.

Bedtime stories!.

CHAPTER EIGHT

After the funeral was over I returned to the flat. In the evening, when all Mothers friends and relatives had gone home, I sat down to take stock of my situation. I thought I had done my duty to my Mother and helped her through all her trials and tribulations, provided a home for her in England and was her constant companion through the war. To me she was a rock, once she had made up her mind to do something, nothing would stand in the way. She was an inspiration to me. If I could be so positive about everything I would be very pleased.

The flat was empty and I wandered from room to room trying to collect my thoughts and wondered what I would do in the future. I was now alone. I had no one to worry about. My brain was in turmoil. The flat was secure. In the next few days I sorted Mothers personal things and stored them away, the only thing I kept out was the wedding day picture of Mother and Father. They looked so smart and happy, it was a pity things did not turn out better for them.

During the winter I visited Rose and Sidney at their farm and was able to go with Rose on a short stay in Bournemouth. St Georges Hotel was very comfortable, looking out to sea towards the Isle of Wight and the Dorset coast. I liked it beside the sea, it was so refreshing and the smell of salt in the air always did me good. We discussed many things when we were sitting in the lounge in the winter sun and looking out to sea. I told Rose my inner thoughts and a recurring idea about travelling in Europe. There was so much to see and I wanted to sample the culture of European cities. Rose commented that there was nothing to stop me now that I was on my own. But could I afford it? Constant travel would be costly. We discussed it no more. I returned to Oxford to dwell on my future. I realised I was a restless character and nothing pleased me more than to be moving to different situations.

It was during October that I thought about a plan that would allow me to travel and at the same time to earn money. Perhaps if I advertised I would get some reaction. "The Lady" magazine always had adverts requiring companions and nannies to look after small children. Perhaps I should try this approach. I therefore inserted an advert saying that a "Canadian young lady, fluent in English and French, well educated, seeks position of trust with Continental family. Some experience with young children". Perhaps that would do the trick.

After very much thought I at last came to the conclusion that I should give my notice in to my employers, who had been so very good to me for so long. I therefore gave them one months notice according to my employment contract. Having done this I discussed it with all my friends and, in the meantime, the Oxford University Women's Appointments Committee very kindly sent me a reference.

To whom it may concern

16th November 1949.

Miss M.R.Pyniger has served as the Assistant Secretary of this Committee from August 1946 to the present time. During this period she has been responsible for the running of a small office and for secretarial work. She is now leaving at her own request.

She and I started our work for this Committee at the same time, both of us being new to this particular kind of work. Owing to my predecessors illness, we inherited considerable arrears. Miss Pyniger attacked her job with very great energy and goodwill. She proved to be a fast worker and she took a keen intelligent interest in the problems involved.

Her special strength, however, lies in her dealings with people. Large numbers of graduates and undergraduates visit this office and Miss Pyniger has proved an excellent receptionist, with a retentive memory for their individual circumstances and a gift for establishing friendly contacts with them. She had proved very successful in training the junior shorthand typist who worked under her supervision. I can recommend Miss Pyniger for a responsible supervisory post involving personal relationships.

Doris Fone.

Secretary.

Mabel also received a personal letter of thanks from the Rector of Lincoln College dated 18th November 1949.

Dear Miss Pyniger.

The Women's Appointments Committee at their meeting on Friday November 11th, instructed me to write to you and express our appreciation of the way you have helped us and the interest that you have taken in our work. We are very sorry that you have decided to take up some other position but send you our best wishes for your success and happiness in whatever you decide to do.

Yours sincerely,

Kath Murray.

Several days later I was talking to my friend Betty when her mother said that she had been talking to her friend at No 84 Windmill Road who had received a letter from a friend of hers in Belgium. A certain Mr Marbach, who had recently suffered the loss of his wife, they had adopted a little girl from England and he was finding it difficult to look after her and see to his business. He was considering looking for a housekeeper/ governess to look after his house and child.

I was, of course quite interested in this information and discussed it with Mrs Twinning to find out more about Mr Marbach. She found out that Mrs Twinning's friend had known the Marbachs a long time and could confirm that they were genuine. Mrs Twining agreed to write to Belgium and explain that she knew of a person who perhaps would be interested in that kind of situation. After several exchange of letters it was agreed that I should go to Belgium for an interview.

The Marbachs lived at No 22 Rue des Moineaux, Ghent where I duly presented myself. Mr Marbach answered the doorbell and welcomed me to his house. He showed me into the sitting room and asked me to take a seat. He spoke in English but said that he usually spoke in French when at business. He inquired whether I was able to speak French well. I said I could but with a Canadian accent. Mr Marbach laughed and said I would no doubt lose that in due course. He explained the situation and asked why I thought I could fulfil his requirements. I explained that I was used to doing housework and that when in Canada I had considerable experience in looking after small girls in the Brownies.

Mr Marbach was particularly interested in the various references and school achievements that I had produced. He commented that she certainly had a lot of experience in office routines but was most interested in the comments about her being able to get along with people and to understand their personal situations. He showed me around the house including the room that would be mine if I was appointed. The house was quite large and typical of Belgian architecture and well appointed with antique furniture. He then explained what he thought would be my duties; I would not have to clean as that was done by a lady coming in each day; I would however be responsible to see that it was done satisfactory and to organise the household routines; I would have to cook meals in the morning and evening, but above all to look after his adopted daughter, see to her education, help with her homework and accompany her to and from school each day. In short, to be her companion in the absence of a mother.

His daughter had been adopted from the U.K. Her name was Antoinette Mary Marbach, known to the household and her friends as Nennette. She was six years old and attended the local state school.

Mr Marbach suggested that I stayed for tea when she could meet Nennette when he collected her that afternoon. It was quite obvious that he wanted her and Nenette to spend some time together to get some idea of their individual reactions to each other.

At the appointed time Mr Marbach took me in the car to pick her up. He introduced me to her and they returned to the house. Nennette was a pretty blond girl with hair down to her shoulders. Very neat with her clothes and very well spoken. I spent the rest of the day with her just talking about her school and telling her about England and Canada. Bedtime came and I told her some stories that I had related to the Brownies in Winnipeg.

Mr Marbach suggested that I should stay on for a few days, in order that they both could think about whether they were compatible. I, of course, agreed and stayed another three days. Nennette asked me what my full name was and when I told her she said she would like to call me "Pinnie", short for Pyniger. That name stuck with me for the rest of my life. At the end of my stay Mr Marbach asked me how I felt about the position, he said that he was quite happy to employ me if I thought that I would be happy in Ghent.

There is no doubt that this was just what I wanted, a new start, a new place, new surroundings and new challenges, I would be able to leave my old life behind and start afresh. After my salary had been agreed I made the monumental decision to accept the position. I was free. It was agreed that I would return to Oxford to clear my flat. I made arrangements for the storage of my furniture that I did not wish to sell. Cousin Rose took most of the items because their house was large enough to store it without cost.

I had been working in the U.K. for some time now and I did not want to stop contributing to my state pension. I therefore asked my bank to pay my contributions from my account while I was out of the country working. Whether this was a sign that I was not completely sure that my decision to go to Europe to work was the right one, I shall never know. I was, however, hedging my bets.

After a round of visits to all my friends to say goodbye, I returned to Ghent to start my new life. I threw myself into the situation with gusto, my daily routine began with breakfast with the family in the English fashion, then off to school on the bus with Nennette, back home to see the "daily" and attend to the other jobs about the house. Mid afternoon I was back to school to collect Nennette and return home to help her with homework. At 6 p.m. it was dinnertime with the three of us seated round the dining room table. We then talked about the days events and perhaps made some arrangements for the weekends. Mr Marbach was very friendly and appeared to appreciate my efforts to help Nennette. It did not take me long to get used to the daily routine, studying my mothers old cookery book to find ideas for different recipes to make dinnertimes more interesting.

Time seemed to pass very quickly and before long it was Christmas. I, for the first time, was able to enjoy the seasonal festivities through the eyes of a child. The decorations, the lights and the anticipation of presents on Christmas day. Ghent was beautiful at this time of year and when the school holidays started they toured the City to see all the magnificent window displays and sample some of the very tasty chocolate at which the Belgians excel. We decorated the house and erected a Christmas tree with its usual decorations. Christmas day came and Nennette and I enjoyed the opening of her presents, in was great fun. Mr Marbach invited his friend around for an evening party. I thoroughly enjoyed myself and after putting Nennette to bed was able to join in the conversations with the guests. Mr Marbach introduced me as Pinnie and I was accepted as part of the family.

During the whole of the Christmas period I had not been able to attend Church. I was disappointed about this, so much so that I resolved to speak to Mr Marbach about my taking time off to attend services and also about Nennettes religious upbringing. When the opportunity arose I asked him what he wished me to do. I made it quite plain that I would like to attend services regularly and perhaps if he had no objections I could take Nennette along with me. They were both of the Anglican faith so there was no problem. Mr Marbach said he had no objections to my proposal but said that if Nennette appeared not to appreciate the services she was not to be forced.

The local Anglican Church was not far away and the following Sunday we went to the morning service where we met many new people who were to become my friends. As usual when English people are abroad they tend to form friendly circles and visit their houses for tea and to discuss events at home. Nennette usually went with me on these occasions and therefore made many young friends in the bargain. I made it plain that my devotion to the Anglican faith, inspired by my experience in Canada, was the prime motive in my life but I never thrust it upon anyone else; if they wished to talk about it I was happy to do so.

Life at the Marbachs continued in the same pattern, I was happy and the daily routines seemed to sort themselves out very well, so much so that I found there was time to explore different avenues of interest. One such interest was the Opera House, Koninklijke Opera van Gent, where I went as often as possible as music and dancing became one of my delights. Occasionally Mr Marbach would accompany us and, in fact, as the year went on he took us to many beautiful parts of Belgium and we became quite good friends. One year I suggested they should come with me to visit my relatives in the U.K. Mr Marbach thought it a great idea. And in due course we went and stayed with cousin Rose and Sidney on their farm in Hampshire. From there we then on to London where I showed them the sights of the city. They all stayed at the Commonwealth Club where I was a member.

1950 passed with me as usual writing to all and sundry about my activities in Belgium. One letter went to the Hydro Electric Company in Winnipeg, congratulating Mr J.W. Sanger on his retirement at a party at the Fort Garry Hotel. I had worked with him during my employment with the Company.

My relationship with Nennette went from strength to strength, the household was happy and contented and the family continued with our visits to many attractions such as to the beautiful City of Spa in the Ardenne. Here I took "The Waters" and declared it did my feet and legs a world of good. I was in the habit of walking everywhere and at a great pace, so much so that most people asked me to slow down, they said that a day out with Pinnie made everyone very tired. Of course, in Winnipeg you had to walk everywhere as we could not afford the tram fare. My motto of "Nothing for the dumb" stood me in good stead, at the best 4 star hotels I would drag everyone in passed the uniformed doormen declaring that we all wanted a good cup of tea. Most times I had the waiters running at my beck and call.

It was during 1951 that Mr Marbach introduced a lady-friend into the household. We were to call her Aunt Sine. She was a teacher. I accepted the situation as I was bound to do, but most people thought that I secretly resented the intrusion into the family. I had worked up a good relationship with everyone and this would seem to undermine it if I was not careful. However, silence is golden, and this is what I did.

The following year Mr Marbach and Aunt Sine were married. This situation worried me quite a lot. Mrs Marbach quite rightly now had the household to do with as she pleased. She was not overbearing or difficult, in fact just the reverse, she was kind and understanding of my position. I liked her a lot, but of course I could not organise the household as I had in the past. I continued with my work in the house and continued to help Nennette as usual with her schoolwork. I could see that Nennette was torn between her allegiance to her stepmother and to me. After a few weeks I decided that this could not go on and I decided to asked Mr and Mrs Marbach to find another governess as I was worried about the situation. They tried to persuade me to change my mind and would be very sorry to lose me and said they were happy with all I had done for Nennette.

Nennette was heartbroken. I think she really loved me and would miss me greatly. The trips to school with Nennette became very sad as we discussed the situation every day. Nennette said she had told some of her classmates that I would be leaving so that one day when the telephone rang for me, I was surprised to speak to a Madame Waks who was the mother of Nennettes school friend. Her daughter had said she was leaving the Marbachs and she wondered if I had found other work and, if not, would I consider coming to live with them to look after her children. I was completely surprised but agreed to go and see her to discuss it.

The Waks family lived quite near the Marbachs in Ghent. Their three children, Danielle, Lydia and David were very young and Madam Waks was 12 years younger than me. This would be a greater challenge as she would have to be a nurse as well as a governess. Mr and Mrs Waks were a delightful couple. Their house was more modern that the Marbachs and the furniture was in keeping with the house. The interview went well, the fact that the children were so young made me dwell on the fact that I was not a trained nurse. But at the age of 45 I had acquired over the years a lot of common sense that no doubt would suffice but, if not sufficient, I would call a Doctor. The fact that the Waks had known about me for some time and had heard all about my capabilities made them keen to employ me. After great thought I agreed to their terms and two weeks latter moved to the Waks household.

I made up my mind never to lose contact with the Marbachs. The children saw each other at school every day and I would visit the Marbachs on a regular basis so there would be no animosity about my leaving. The new position presented new problems, younger children required more attention and I was kept very busy. But with Madam Waks being at home I did not have to worry about the house or cooking. I could not drive a car but Madam Waks took them all out when necessary. By this time I had established a good idea of what interested the children in the City and was always ready to suggest somewhere to go at the weekends. Madam Waks and her husband were always in demand with their business, so that I spent many hours with the children organising games and walks in the countryside, visits to the zoo etc...

At this time I continued in earnest what was to become a lifelong habit of recording my life in diaries and compiling a scrap book, mainly at that time about the British Royal Families.

I wrote about my travels, food, the children and holidays, also about the more mundane things one does every week, the cost of hairdressing etc... As usual I wrote letters to everyone that prompted a great number of replies. I received invitations to visit my friends when I was in the U.K. or Canada if I should return one day. My life with the Waks family continued very satisfactory, my relationship with all the children was good and spent many happy hours with them, everything was going as planned.

Christmas 1951 was a very enjoyable occasion. The Waks family house was decorated beautifully, the Christmas lunch was cooked by Madam Waks with my help, the table was full of the most delicious food. Afterwards, in my room, I was able to listen on the radio; King George VI gave his Christmas message to all the people in the U.K. and the Commonwealth. I never missed an opportunity to listen to or read articles in the newspapers about Royalty. My scrapbook was full of press cuttings about them.

The New Year 1952 started with heavy falls of snow that took me and the children out to enjoy rides on the sledge and skating on the frozen lakes. The 6th of February brought sad news, King George VI died. It was headlines of course, all over the U.K. and on the Radio. I knew he did not enjoy good health and had noticed lately in pictures of him in the press that his face was very drawn. The last picture I saw of him was waving goodbye to his daughter Elizabeth and her husband Prince Phillip on their departure to South Africa for an official visit. The Belgian newspaper in Ghent, "La Flanders Liberal", devoted Front Page news of the sad occasion with pictures of the King and announcing that Princess Elizabeth at the age of 26 would be proclaimed Queen if the King should die. Unfortunately the king did die and I immediately sat down and wrote a letter to the now Queen Mother, saying how sad I was to hear the news and hoped she would continue with her public good work. All English people loved her and I said I would be praying for her during the coming months. I was surprised to receive a reply from Buckingham Palace acknowledging my letter and thanking me for my good wishes; signed by her Personal Secretary. I kept all the press cuttings of the state funeral in London, expressing surprise that King Baudouin of the Belgians was not there.

It was announced in Ghent that a special service of commemoration would be held at The Dutch Reformed Church, Brabantdam, Ghent, on Sunday 17th February 1952 at 11.30 a.m. I wrote off at once for a ticket. I just had to pay my respects to a great King who had stayed in London during all the air raids on London and like me had been bombed. On the appointed day I was in my seat in the Church with many of the British and Commonwealth dignitaries living in Belgium. At 11.30 a.m. there was no sign of King Baudouin, who eventually arrived 10 minutes late. A section of the crowd booed him as he entered. He was welcomed by the Chaplain the Rev Sir Charles Bentick. After the service all British people were invited for coffee in the public hall next to the Church. Here I talked to members of the British Diplomatic Corps in Belgium. I could not understand the animosity that existed between the British and Belgian Royal Families. It was something to do with King Baudouins refusal to attend King George's funeral in London.

Back to the house and into her routine as governess to the three small children, I was very much aware of the standard of living in Belgium, they did not seem to be short of anything , whereas in Britain they were still experiencing rationing of some items. Cousin Rose wrote to say it was still difficult to get some groceries and tropical fruit was not available at all. This was six years after the war! Britain had really exhausted her financial situation trying to save democracy for the world.

After Easter Madam Waks said that they were planning a holiday in Austria. She asked me to go along to help out with the children. Glory be! I said, what wonderful news. All the children were so pleased to be going to a foreign country, what fun. They could not wait. Early July the family set off to the

Schlosshotel, Velden, am Worthersee, Austria. The hotel was situated beside a lake. There they enjoyed bathing, boating and walking in the beautiful mountains. I received two postcards from Nennette indicating that their friendship was as strong as ever.

Dear Pinnie.
23rd July 1952

How are you? I hope you are well. Daddy and I are going to the farm next Friday 25th by plane. How is Lydia and Auntie Gerty ? the daddy of Lydia and Danielle. Here it is quite nice, Annie left last Saturday. How is it in Austria. I think Lydia and Danielle are getting on fine. I went to a faire and won a teddy bear. He or she is very nice.

Kind regards from Tante Sine and bobonne {the dog} and Daddy.

Love from Nennette.

Back home to Ghent at the beginning of August after a wonderful holiday, I had received an invitation to the wedding of Roses second son Kenneth, to Audrey whom I had met at their farm and later came to stay with me in Oxford. I liked her very much as she had an independent philosophy of life and was determined to succeed in everything she did by her own efforts. Unfortunately I could not go as I had just returned from Austria and I could not see my way clear to ask for extra time off. I therefore went out and bought a lovely Brussels lace tablecloth and napkins. I posted them to her with my apologies for not coming.

At the end of September Madam Waks informed me that they would be moving house to the City of Spa in the southern part of Belgium. Great news, another town, different scenery, more friends etc... I would be living at number 9 Avenue Awedle` Herse, Spa.

Spa, as you know, is renowned for its healing waters, discovered by the Romans and developed by the Belgians into a delightful Town. The Bathhouse being a beautiful building in keeping with the rest of the Town. The surrounding countryside is covered with trees and clear streams cascading down to the Town. Walking in this area is the most beautiful that I had experienced so far. The Children loved it. I wrote to all my friends about my change of address. I did not regret my decision to come to Europe to work. Everything was working out as I had planned. I looked forward to many more years with the Waks family. The children were growing up fast and accordingly I was able to arrange outings of a more adult nature. Cross country skiing in the winter, horse riding and long walks in the Ardenne Forest.

The three children were by this time quite difficult to control. They were headstrong but very intelligent and they caused me to be exhausted at the end of the day. However, I soldiered on hoping that things would get better.

One day Madam Waks said that the family would be taking another holiday in Marbella, at Puerto Banes and would she come along? I said I would be pleased to come. This holiday proved to be very delightful as the weather was warm and sunny all day, sea bathing every day was a must for the children and this enabled me to rest in the sun while keeping an eye on them.

Returning home to Spa, the routine continued as usual until Mr Waks told me that they might be moving to San Paulo in Brazil. This was, of course, in relation to his business. This was a shock for me as I had not anticipated any move out of

Europe. I thought about this for some time and came to the conclusion that while I would go if pressed I would rather find alternative employment.

The following day, quite by coincidence, I received a letter from Morveth in London to say that she had secured a position with The World Council of Churches in Geneva. She would be taking up the position on the first of the following month. Would I like to come and visit her as she had secured an apartment large enough for two people. Glory be! The Lord works in curious ways. This was just what she wanted. I would go to Geneva and look for work there.

The following day I told Madam Waks that I had decided not to come to Brazil with them but would go to Geneva where my friend was to be working in future. I said I would stay on for another four weeks. I looked forward to going but was sad that I was leaving the children. I had created such a good relationship with them that I regarded them as my own. Nennette was particularly sad as they had such a lot in common with England. Many tears were shed during those weeks and on the very day that I was to leave Madam Waks told me that the arrangements to go to Brazil had all been cancelled, they would stay where they were. Oh dear! What should I do? After all the arrangements I had made I felt I could not go back and decided go to Geneva as planned. All the family and Nennette came to the station to see me off. More tears, hugs and kisses, all promised to keep in touch.

In my scrapbook I wrote, no doubt after the farewell:-

A Recipe for Friendship. 1952.

Take one pound of double refined sincerity with two ounces of constancy and a sprig of evergreen memory, sweeten it with a little good glamour throwing in a large quantity of good nature. Keeping it stirring with good sense that it may not boil too fast. When it is grown to a hard substance take it off, and let it stand a year, then try it by the fire of affliction, if that does not dissolve it, you may be sure it is well made and will last as long as you will have it.

Arriving in Geneva station I was met by Morveth, who took me to her flat overlooking the Airport. The flat was in a suburb of Geneva called Petit Sacconex, with an excellent bus service straight into the city centre. I had not seen Morveth since I had left London, we had a lot to talk about. After settling in, the two of us set about exploring the city. It was so different from anything we had experienced before. Very cosmopolitan with people from all over the World, most of them working at the United Nations. The view from the waterfront in the city overlooking Lake Leman towards the Alps, was dramatic with the world renowned water jet reaching far up over the lake. It was winter but the flat was very warm and the two of us settled down to a very different life.

Morveth suggested that I advertised in the local papers for a position as governess similar to the one that she put in the Lady Magazine in England. This they did and received a response from a Mr Bela, who lived in the small village of Caux, high up above Montreux at the eastern end of Lake Leman. He was looking for a responsible person to look after his children while he and his wife were away abroad on business. The four children were aged 3, 6, 8 and 11. He was a very high powered businessman who had interests in the meat industry in South and North America plus London. He travelled to these places often.

I went for an interview and I was seen by Mrs Bela herself, their house was situated in the village of Caux high up in the mountains at the eastern end of the lake. I took the funicular railway from Montreux to the village. Mrs Bela was a lovely lady and I immediately liked her. The youngest child, aged 3, was in the nursery playing while the others were at school.

They discussed the situation at great length although at no time did I see the other children. Her room would be at the top of the house with a window overlooking the lake and the Alps on the left. It was the most magnificent view that one could imagine. My job would be to look after the children at home and to see to their schooling, the salary was very satisfactory, she would have no cooking unless she wanted to, and a car was available with a driver when I took the children out. I asked if I could think about this offer and would contact Mrs Bela within two days.

On returning to Geneva I discussed the situation with Morveth, going over the problems which might occur. I was worried about there being four children. I had not anticipated such a large family. At least two of the children were old enough not to require individual attention. I decided to accept the situation and informed Mrs Bela accordingly. I started work with the family on 1st November 1952.

CHAPTER NINE

I packed all my worldly goods, said goodbye to Morveth and took a taxi to the central station in Geneva. Twenty minutes latter the train drew in and I looked for a seat on the side where I could view the beautiful lake Leman during my journey. The route was all along the lake edge and I looked forward to seeing it during the summer when all the trees were in bloom.

Too soon I arrived in Montreux, transferred to the funicular train that ran up to the summit of the Rocher de Naye mountain. Caux was about halfway up, the track rose very steeply and I soon had a magnificent view of the lake and the French Alps on my left in the High Savoy. Caux was a small village but its situation was unique, all the houses had a superb view and were mostly occupied by wealthy people. The Bela residence was no exception, a well built house with a beautiful garden. At the rear was a field where I was told was used for sledging in the snow. I settled into my room and started work at once.

My first job was to see to the smallest child, taking her out for a walk using the time to familiarise myself with the surrounding area. The funicular railway ran fairly regularly through the village, each time stopping in the station to allow another train to pass on the way down. We stopped to watch the people getting on and off and had a nice cup of tea in the station buffet. I returned to the house for lunch with Mrs Bela when we had the opportunity to discuss many details of my job. Then off we went in the car down to Montreux to collect the other children from school. There were three other children, all full of life and were keen to see who mother had employed to look after them.

The 11 year old quized me about my name and where I had come from. After much whispering and laughter they all agreed to call me by the now accepted name of Pinnie. They were excited to learn that I was born in Canada and had been out on the prairies living with real red Indians, and all about London and especially the Royal Palaces. The journey home was all chatter and Mrs Bela thought it was a good sign that we would get on well together.

The household spoke in two languages, French and English, they used whichever came to mind first. This did not worry me at all. The household routines were the same as I had been used to; get up, wash and dress the children, give them their breakfast and take then to school, come back and see to the baby and do whatever was necessary for the children when they returned. Lunch at midday and then down to the school to pick up the other three and bring them safely home.

The evenings were spent indoors due to the bad weather and deep snow, doing homework and playing board games. Story telling was very popular as the days went on I found that sometimes the children found it difficult to put their coats on the right way. I persevered to teach them the correct way but met with little success. I thought this a little odd.

I soon discovered that Mr and Mrs Bela were very well educated judging by their conversation and opinions about world affairs. I thought they had an IQ far in advance of most people, it was said they were both professors, but I never mentioned the subject as it was only conjecture.

Christmas came and went with the household enjoying all the usual celebrations. January 1953 saw the children returning to school. My daily trip with the children down to Montreux became an interesting part of the day. Outside the school I met other governesses also bringing their children to the same school and therefore struck up a friendship with some of them. The area we were in was renowned for the residence of wealthy people from all over the world. It was said Switzerland was a tax haven for them. I did not know, all I wanted was a happy life and somewhere nice to live. I certainly had both of that here.

I was able to attend the Anglican Church of "All Saints" in Vevey most Sundays. I was convinced the "Lord would look after me". I also applied for a work permit from the Swiss authorities and in due course it was granted, renewable every three years. I gave my official home as the address of my cousin Rose in England. The weather during January was cold and the snow at Caux was very deep. I spent a lot of time with the children out in the field near the house, sledging, snowballing and building snowmen. The real treat was to go on the funicular further up the track to the summit through snow laden trees and boulders, through tunnels and out in the sunshine above the clouds at the top there was a restaurant where they could enjoy lots of their favourite food and ice cream. During the summer they could explore the Alpine Gardens near at hand.

I was becoming worried that the children still found it difficult to grasp the most simple problems that they had been set for their home-work. I tried to spend as much time as possible working hard on this problem and wondering if they were finding work at school as difficult. Not all the children were the same; one would find a problem difficult and another easy. Perhaps it was me, did I have enough patience? I must try harder.

During late February Mrs Bela told me that she and her husband would be leaving shortly to go to Argentina on business. They would away for about 4 weeks, I would be in charge of the household, with the help of the chauffeur/gardener, who lived in an adjoining cottage and the daily cook/cleaner. This would be the first great challenge for me. The time came and I accepted the responsibilities with some misgivings. I discussed the situation with some of my friends when I was at the school. They gave me encouragement and advice. There would be no time off at all, I was in charge the whole time, night and day. Each day brought some difficulties but I overcame them with renewed energy, being firm but kind to the children. March brought an easing of the cold weather that helped a lot as we were able get outside much more often. Colds and flu took their toll and the Doctor was called in more that once.

I found my time completely taken up with the children, they were sometimes intolerable. I decided to take the matter up with the school head teacher. When I saw her I managed to speak to her, she said she knew of these problems and was of the opinion that they were in need of specialist teaching at another school. She said that her appraisal would be documented in the children's reports that the parents would receive in due course. The parents would then decide what to do. I was relieved as I should not be seen as interfering.

The four weeks went by and at the end I was very pleased to have the children's mother back home. The school run became a daily welcome break and sometimes I would spend a little time with a particular lady who I had heard talking to another governess in a broad Scottish accent. I cultivated this friendship and looked forward to meeting her every day. As our friendship matured, on the odd time when our days off coincided, we would occasionally meet for coffee and perhaps a little personal shopping in Montreux. Her name was Edith McKenzie, a dour Scot if ever there was one. Our friendship grew and I was pleased to tell her about my problems with the children, I received good advice from her and put it into practice when necessary. I was very thankful for this acquaintance as she had helped me a lot.

June 2nd 1953 dawned overcast with a threat of rain, this was the day that I had set aside to listen on the radio to the BBC World Service commentary of the crowning of Princess Elizabeth as Queen of the U.K. and the Commonwealth of Nations; the programme was from Westminster Abbey in London. The children were at school so that I couldst listen without interruption. I was a devoted admirer of the Royal Family and was determined not to miss a minute of the broadcast. The Archbishop of Canterbury, Dr Fisher took the service and presented the Princess to her people as their future undoubted Queen. The Queen turning north, south, east and west replied by bowing slightly.

The commentator described the scene in the Abbey, full to the brim with colour from the robes of the nobility and flowers. When the crown was put on her head they all cried out "GOD SAVE THE QUEEN". Trumpet fanfares rang out one after the other. The Queen was accompanied by her husband Prince Phillip, who it was announced had been made Duke of Edinburgh.

At last the ceremony was over and I sat down to write to the Queen, telling her how much I had enjoyed the service from the Cathedral, assuring her of my undying allegiance and support, wishing her good health and happiness in the years to come.

Summer came and with it the blooming of the mountain flowers, walks along the narrow mountain paths through the trees and over the little streams that tumbled down to the lake. It was idyllic. Mrs Bela went away for another 4 weeks on business, again I was in charge. I found it just as tiring as before although I managed quite well but was pleased when it came to an end. Mrs Bela had received the children reports but had not said a word about their lack of progress. I thought it odd that in spite of the parents being so well educated their children were afflicted with an inability to grasp the most simple tasks. There must have been a breakdown of the genes inherited from their parents. During the summer holidays I took the children down to Montreux and Lausanne to visit the zoo and other attractions. I began to think that I had made a mistake in taking this position, I loved the children and would do nothing to hurt their feelings but I found it quite impossible at times.

Edith and I would regularly meet on a Sunday when attending church at Vevey. There were a great number of British residents in the area as well as people living in the locality who were from Commonwealth Countries, many from central Africa. There were many social associations and organisations catering for these people, most of the members would get notices of forthcoming events in the area. They were surprised to learn that about a week after the Coronation in London, they were all invited to a Coronation Celebration in the Montreux- Vevey area; "Glory be!" I said, I am not going to miss that! It was to be held at the All Saints Church at 4 o'clock in Montreux. The Church was decorated with flags of all Commonwealth countries together with beautiful flowers arranged around a huge portrait of the Queen and her husband, the Duke of Edinburgh.

The service was conducted by the resident vicar aided by another clergyman from Geneva. A senior member of the English diplomatic Corps from the United Nations gave an address, explaining that the Coronation is a public declaration of a solemn covenant between the Queen and her peoples, but it is also on our part a sign of loyalty. The Coronation service itself implies that the life of the Monarch is a life dedicated to her peoples. After the service the band of the Kursaal played a selection of music of traditional airs. Including Land of Hope and Glory, Roses of Picardy, Londonderry air and Drink to me only with thine eyes. Tea and cakes were provided ending with the Royal Toast and the National Anthem. It was a beautiful afternoon, one which I would remember all my life.

Duty called back at Caux. I continued with my struggle to teach the children table manners amongst other necessary things for educated children. It was an uphill struggle but I persevered. My friendship with Edith strengthened so much so that one day while I was at home I received a phone call from a lady who said she was the employer of Edith and was concerned that she appeared to be very lonely. She had spoken about me and how their friendship had developed and matured. Would I consider having a grand day out with her, do personal shopping, go to any first class restaurant for an evening meal, go by taxi, she would pay all the bills for both of them. This took me rather back, may I ask who is calling; Oh, I am sorry, it is Mrs Chaplin from the Manoir, Corsier-sur-Vevey............ Glory be! Could it be THE MRS OONA CHAPLIN, wife of Charlie?

It took me a few moments to get my senses back but I readily agreed and said that I would try to arrange a day out when I next met Edith. And so it came about that we did have a day together and enjoyed every moment of it, spending it in Lausanne. Edith told me that everyone at the Manoir called her KK, at least that's what the children called her, from that moment on I also called her KK.

It was during July that I gave great thought to whether I should continue in this job. I tried my best but was getting nowhere. In fact, I thought that I was doing the children a disservice by staying. They really ought to be at a specialist school. I reluctantly asked to discuss it with their parents. I put my case and said I ought to leave as soon as possible, or at least until they had recruited another Governess. They begged me to stay but I had made up my mind and stood my ground. After leaving I had decided to go back to England for a prolonged visit, therefore I worked up until 15th September 1953 and then packed my bags for England.

Mr George Bela gave me the following reference dated 15th September 1953:-

To whom it may concern.

Miss Mabel Pyniger entered our household on November 1st 1952 and stayed with us until this date, looking after our four children aged 11, 8, 6 and 3 with competence and affection.

She also took charge of the entire household during our frequent journeys abroad. She is not afraid of responsibility and possesses tact, loyalty and great charm of manner, these qualities contributing greatly to the happy atmosphere of the house.

Signed by **George Bela.**

One of the greatest moments of unhappiness in my life occurred several months after I had left the Bela household. Mrs Bela and her children, together with the new Nannie, were leaving Caux for Montreux in the car when on one of the very dangerous steep hairpin bends in the road they were involved in an accident with another car resulting in the death of the Nannie and three children.

After staying one night with my great friend Morveth in Geneva, I caught a flight to London and a train south to Portsmouth where my cousin Rose picked me up in her car and took me back to their farm in the Meon Valley. It was nice to be back where I did not have to remember I was an employee. I could say what I pleased, everyone called me Mabel in England and it seemed strange to be called by my proper name. I set about visiting all my relatives living nearby; cousin Nellie at Southwick village, cousin Tinnie at Portchester and their daughters. A short holiday with Rose was arranged in Bournemouth at the St Georges Hotel, overlooking the sea. It was great, the air was invigorating and the Hotel comfortable with a typical English bar. I was so pleased for the break, Rose and I talked about almost everything including news about the forthcoming birth of a baby to Audrey and Ken in the new year.

While at Bournemouth I took advantage to go to Poole to visit a very old friend from London days, Dorothy Bevan. She had recently bought a property there. Then back home to the farm and then off to Nottingham to see my Auntie Daisy and cousin Phillip. I stayed two days and returned to London to see Auntie Mabel. Uncle William had died a few years previously. I stayed three days with them, taking tea of course at Fortnum and Masons. From London I went on to Coulsdon in Surrey to see another friend, Mrs Oliver. I left there on 12th November and returned home to the farm of Rose and Sydney. Here I caught up with my letter writing to most of my friends in Canada. I was planning a visit there the following year 1954. I had had so many invitations that I felt I could not put them off any longer. I had written in a provisional date of July 54 – Jan 55.

One day, while sitting in front of a roaring wood log fire I looked up and saw a red Royal Mail post van coming down the front drive. The driver delivered a **telegram** (Authors Note : the original remains in my possession) for me from the main post office in Fareham where it had been redirected from Coulsdon, Surrey. It was from KK in Switzerland from the home of Mr and Mrs Charles Chaplin at Corsier-sur-Vevey.

"CAN YOU COME OVER AND HELP OUT WITH THE CHILDREN FOR TWO OR THREE MONTHS".

Glory be!. I was so surprised to receive this request I just sat down to make sure what I was reading was real. Look at this Rose, I said, What shall I do? I discussed it over lunch and finally decided to wire back saying "ON MY WAY". I knew this was a cry for help. KK was getting nervous. Mrs Chaplin was expecting a new baby any time now, she wanted help with the older ones; the new baby came along safely on time and was named Eugene Anthony, their second son.

A flight was arranged as soon as possible to Geneva and I went straight to the Manoir where they lived overlooking Vevey. A large turn of the century house, painted all white with a veranda running all along the southern aspect. It was above the town of Vevey, standing in about 14 hectares of parkland with mature trees planted with great care not to obstruct the view over the lake and mountains beyond. It was here that Mr and Mrs Chaplin had decided to make their home after they had been refused permission to return to the U.S.A. The huge iron gates were locked and I rang the bell provided. There was a gatehouse, or lodge, quite near and a gentleman came out to inquire my business. I told him I had an appointment with KK and Mrs Chaplin, whereupon he escorted me to the rear entrance. He opened the door and gave a shout for KK. She welcomed me with open arms.

KK took me into the staff quarters and sat me down. How glad I am to see you, she said, I'm nearly at my wits end. We need more help in the house to look after the older children. The new baby is quite enough for me. Mrs Chaplin authorised me to wire you to see if would come to help out for a short while. She wants to see you as soon as you arrive. After a nice cup of tea we went along to the drawing room to see her. Mrs Chaplin was a beautiful person, quite young and easy to talk to. She reiterated what KK had said and asked me if I would stay until she had got used to another baby. She suggested that I took charge of the older children and leave the young one to KK.

She would have her own room facing south. She would not be responsible for any housework or cooking and a chauffeur would be on hand when required. She also suggested a reasonable salary but said that she would required to work very closely with KK in all matters as she had been with them for a very long time in America and knew all the problems.

What did I think? This was the ultimate that I had aspired to when I had decided to work in Europe. Mrs Chaplin spoke for some time about the need for maximum security, at no time were the children to be out of my sight; the McCarthy purges in America were still going on, the possibility of kidnapping was very real. She should use the family cars whenever possible and always tell someone where they were going. I thought about my decision to visit Canada later on in 1954. I told Mrs Chaplin about my plans but she said I would only be required for a short period and then I would be free. I readily agreed to Mrs Chaplin's terms and started work that very day. Little did I know it but this was the start of a period in my working life that was to transform my attitude to theatre and cinema personalities. I was to meet many international stars, travel the world, see all the wonderful places that I had only dreamed of in the past.

Christmas 1953 was a real treat for all the family. The children that I was responsible for were Geraldine age 10, Michael aged 8 and Josephine aged 5. Victoria aged 3 and the new baby Eugene would the responsibility of KK. The youngest children always slept downstairs next to their parent's bedroom on the first floor and as they got older they moved up to the top floor next to KK and myself.

Amongst the jobs that I was expected to do was to try to educate them about the various festivals during the year. Therefore we set about making advent calendars, explaining to them what it was all about. We then put them on the wall in their bedrooms. A fir tree was brought in from the garden and we all set to and decorated it putting on the lights that made it look so pretty. Mother and Father approved of our efforts and we looked forward to Christmas day. Many presents were hidden away, waiting for the great day.

Christmas lunch table was groaning under the weight of many recipes and decorations. All the food was beautifully prepared by Mary the cook for the occasion. Streamers and crackers were littered about the table and everyone in turn sang a song including Mr and Mrs Chaplin; his was very funny and amused us all. KK and I were privileged that day to eat with all the family, only afterwards were the children allowed to open their presents to great shouts of joy. Afternoon tea was served late at about 5,30 p.m. after which Mr Chaplin suggested that all grown ups should partake in a little dram of Scotch whiskey and soda. From that time onwards whenever Mr Chaplin was in residence he always sent a whiskey and soda into KK's and my room. It was a very nice gesture.

February came along with heavy falls of snow. Mrs Chaplin suggested that they all go skiing at Gstaad. Wonderful! I packed the three children's bags and off we went by train booking into a good hotel. We spent two weeks enjoying horse sleigh rides, ice skating and learning to ski on the children's slopes. We returned to Vevey on the famous Montreux Oberland Bernois mountain railway. Mrs Chaplin had given me a pair of her old but very warm snow boots that were greatly appreciated.

Thursday was the day off for Mary the cook, and on that day Mrs Chaplin usually did the cooking when she was home. She used to provide some of the recipes she had picked up in America, it made a change from the usual and I contributed by making my upside down pineapple cake.

Late February the family were to go to London on business connected with Mr Chaplin's new film. Off we all went by Cadillac and Rolls Royce to Geneva airport where we were shown into the VIP lounge before boarding our plane. We were booked into the Savoy Hotel in London. The next morning Mrs

Chaplin burst into our rooms saying she could not find the film script. Was it packed? Mr Chaplin was furious. Glory be! Why was it always our fault? I said I would telephone home to see where it was and sure enough it was in the studio were Mr Chaplin always worked. The staff dispatched it at once but it took three days to arrive. Oh dear, we survived three days of silence when you could have cut the air.

I used this time to show the children around London, taking a taxi cab to all the usual sights, museums, palaces and Government buildings. I had realised by this time that Mr Chaplin was a little difficult when things were not going as planned. When he was working at home everyone had to tiptoe past his door. No noise! Also when in the garden, everyone had to keep well clear of his window. His friend Jerry Epstein from Hollywood was staying at the Manoir helping with the script and music for the new film. He was a much younger man but had the experience with all new techniques in film making.

Film personalities would come and go in this household with great regularity. We, as staff, were required to pander to their individual whims and fancies. Some I liked and some I did not. One day who should arrive from America but Mr Chaplin's eldest son by his first marriage, his name was Sidney Chaplin. He brought gifts for all the children and I found him very kind and agreeable. He stayed for two weeks and on leaving presented the staff with small presents in appreciation of their efforts to make his stay a memorable one; he gave me an orange Indian silk sari, it was beautiful.

March was Michael's birthday. Presents of a scooter and a gramophone. He was sick after eating too many sweet things at his party. The next day I made him walk to school to do him good; we took Confetti the dog with us.

The next day KK confided in me that she would be leaving soon. I was so shocked I could not believe it. She wanted me to take over from her in the household . I asked her to think about it a bit longer to make sure her decision was final. We talked this over for many days, telling her that I would soon be going to Canada in July, according to the arrangements I had made with Mrs Chaplin. Whether this changed her mind I do not know but later she told me she would be staying. Thank goodness for that. I never knew what the problem was.

The builders moved in to start building a new swimming pool in the garden, it was a grand affair according to the plans, with changing rooms with hot and cold water, towel driers etc. We all looked forward to its completion as this would keep the kids happy for many hours.

Sidney Chaplin came again and brought along his new girl friend Kay Kendall, she had just completed the film "Genevieve" and was cock-a-hoop with its success. Mr Chaplin was not impressed. He again bought presents for all the children. They both signed my autograph book.

On Thursday 18th April, I helped Mrs Chaplin in the kitchen, charcoal steaks were on the menu that day, with all the trimmings. Beautiful. After lunch I went to my room and wrote to the Cunard Shipping Line in Liverpool, England, inquiring about a birth on a boat to Canada. I thought I had better start making my arrangements before someone asked me to do something for the family that I could not refuse.

The following weeks my diary records the usual mundane things, school, shopping etc… Now that the weather had improved we were able to have our children parties out in the garden and many of their friends came to tea including some very local Swiss children. Among these were the Bela children from Caux, my old charges. These events bought home to me how the children mixed with each other with great ease in spite of their quite different cultures. There were some from the local school, the sons of vineyard workers who spoke French in the local dialect using, as I soon discovered, many expletives. Sometimes they would utter these words when Mr

Chaplin was there. He did not speak French so that he did not understand. Trips to mount Peleren and afterwards at St Saphorin for dinner. A beautiful lakeside village restaurant.

Geraldine by this time was attending college in Lausanne, as a weekly boarder, whilst the other school age children still went to the local primary school. It was my job to see them safely there and back. On the 8th May the chauffeur drove me to Lausanne to attend the anniversary church service of the ending of the war. Afterwards I had dinner at Jussy. A small village on the other side of the lake.

The visitors to the Manoir continued to read as entries in Who's Who. My diary for the 18th records a visit from Chrissie and Juliet Coleman, film stars of some fame. Also the Rockefellers and Princess Oblensky from London. The 22nd May Mr and Mrs Sidney Chaplin arrived, [no Kay Kendall] together with Auntie Gipsy, who is Mr Chaplin's sister-in-law. She had a suite at the Beau Rivage Hotel in Lausanne. My job was to introduce all the children to these people and to see that they did not interfere with their stay.

2nd June was a big day. Mr Chaplin received the Peace Prize from the Peace Council. Photographers and Newsmen from all over the world crowded round the Manoir gates asking for interviews and photo shots. Great excitement. The police arrived to keep order. The following day was the "Fete de Narcissus" in the village of Orsonnay. This was the time of the year when all the Narciccus were out in bloom. The whole village was decorated. A carnival of decorated floats completely done with flower petals. It was beautiful.

It was now time for me to arrange with Mrs Chaplin about my leaving for Canada. She said that my work was appreciated, they were more then pleased with the way I had integrated with the children and KK. My original three months had now become six and I had become part of the family. Mrs Chaplin knew that I had arranged this trip and resigned herself to manage without me for some time. But whatever happened they wanted me to come back on a permanent basis. This was indeed good news. I agreed to return as soon as I had completed my itinerary. I said how happy I was with them and thanked her profusely.

My next task was to tell the children that I was leaving for a short holiday. Michael was sad, Jossie and Vicky cried. But I said I would be back and they cheered up a bit and made me promise that I would write regularly. They bought me leaving presents of a Cashmere sweater, slippers, scarf, stockings and perfume.

On 15th June I waved a tearful goodbye, picked up cash from my bank and then George the chauffeur drove me to Geneva Airport on the way pointing out the homes of Madam Paderenski, Chopin's mistress, Madam Standel and the home of Napoleon 1st. I was met in London by Margaret Twining and adjourned to Vegas Restaurant for lunch and then on to St James Park for a walk. We met Ester, my friend from London days who was from Helensburgh in Scotland. I stayed with her overnight and the next day went to the theatre to see Kay Kendal in "Doctor in the House".

Next day after lunch in Fortnums and Masons I went up to Oxford to see Gwyneth and then on to Wickham in Hampshire to visit cousin Rose. I enjoyed strawberries and real cream on the lawn of the old farmhouse joined by Audrey and Ken with their new son, Julian. I had brought a parcel for them of left-off clothes that were too small for Eugene. Audrey was pleased as they were always of good quality. She wanted to hear about all my travels since I had last been at the farm.

July 2nd I sailed for Canada from Southampton. On board the 53.000 ton S.S. United States. I was pleased with such a large cabin but the weather was rough and I could not eat. Sunday 4th I attended a church service with a new friend Mrs McCurran and her daughter Sheena. Gala dinner in the evening in honour of American Independence Day with a lot of streamers and funny hats. Weather reports said it would be dull and warm in the St Lawrence River at Quebec, the temperature was 85 degrees F.

A midnight feast in my cabin and then a movie, "The Moon is Blue".

In the morning, after the customs and pilot boat came alongside, we slowly made our way into Quebec Harbour. I stepped ashore in Canada on 10th July, so hot I had to shed my warm clothes.

CHAPTER TEN

Stepping ashore in Quebec. I was met by two of my old friends from school days, Carol and Margaret. It was strange to hear them calling me Mabel as I had become accustomed to being called Pinnie. As the weather was unusually hot they at once bought ice cream, from the nearest drugstore, then we took a 2 dollar taxi ride to view the City Hall, the famous Chateau, on to the Abraham heights and the fort above the river. Carol then took me back to her flat in the city. Here we just sat and talked. I had a lot to tell them about England, Belgium and Switzerland. It was passed midnight before we went to bed.

The next day being Sunday, I went to communion at St Michaels Church with Carol, who afterwards introduced me to three of her friends, Betty, Paddy and Rita Curran. Paddy took us all in his car to visit the old residential section of the city and the University and during the evening we had dinner with Paddy at his house.

The weather continued to be very hot, and I spent most of my time shopping and taking coffee with Margaret. I must have been very busy as I failed to make any entries in my diaries for the next few days. On 21st July, having enjoyed the friendship and hospitality of my friends, I boarded a train for Winnipeg arriving the next day and being met by Harry Hale and Teresa, friends of Nora Moorhead. They took me to Nora's house where I was to stay.

A grand tour of Winnipeg began the following day. The first stop was at a florist to purchase flowers and then on to St Johns Cathedral to lay them on my fathers grave. I remember kneeling for a few minutes saying in my mind a short prayer; tears were in my eyes when I left the churchyard.

On to my old school Balmoral Hall to see the present Head and look around the new classrooms and then down Westminster Ave to Furby St to see my old house that was looking rather down at heal. Next, on to Landside and Ellis Ave, Carlton and Edmonton St all places where we used to live. In the evening we went down to the Forks and had dinner at a good restaurant overlooking the river.

Next day I visited the Hydro Company offices. A few new faces, same old offices, but the Directors were the same. An impromptu party was convened and a few drinks were consumed; happy memories. I visited the first huge supermarket in Winnipeg, run by a U.K. company called Safeways. In the evening I had dinner with the Moorheads.

According to my diaries my holiday continued with visits to Fort Garry University, Elk Island and the North Shore Mink Ranch.

Saying goodbye to Nora on August 3rd I packed up and took the train to Brandon, Regina and on to Moose Jaw where I had a disgusting meal, cold and uneatable. I refused to pay and left. I continued on to Banff for breakfast and arrived in Vancouver at 9.30 p.m. where I was met by Helen and David. Helen had been a great friend from school days but unfortunately had contacted polio at a very young age. She had struggled with the decease which could not be eradicated and eventually would necessitate the need to use a wheelchair. She had married David under these conditions and they were an ideal couple. He helped her as much as he could, one could say he was a perfect husband. They had a lovely house by the sea on Beach Ave. Here I was invited to stay as long as I wanted and used some of the time helping about the house. Letters from England were waiting for me, giving me all the latest news. As Helen was on holiday we were able to visit many parts of the surrounding area. David used his car to take them through Stanley Park and across the Lions Gate Bridge to West Vancouver arriving at Horseshoe Bay where I paddled in the Pacific Ocean. The weather was beautiful so we had a picnic on the beach. We stayed at the Molasprina Hotel, Kahloke overnight, and back home the following day.

I wrote letters to England and Switzerland as promised and in the afternoon I went to the Bank of Montreal to arrange about some investment with monies I had managed to save. I chose to invest in the South African diamond mines of De Beers. In the evening I went to the cinema and saw a film with Benny Hill; I did not appreciate his humour, I thought him stupid and vulgar. Helen suggested we go to the University Theatre to see "The merry wives of Windsor" - this was much better!

My tour continued with visits to Seattle in the U.S.A, Grouse Mountain, and many other parts of the City. I expressed a wish to visit Vancouver Island and the Capital City of British Columbia, Victoria. This was arranged and we all set off aboard the ferry, Princess Patricia. I thought that Victoria was beautiful, so like England, many of the shops were the same as in London, Marks and Spencers and many more. Red double-decker buses and telephone kiosks. China Town was crowded but they found a space to enjoy a Chinese Meal. Outside the City in the residential area it was just like Surrey in England.

On September 2nd Helens holiday week came to an end and she had to return to their business. They owned a boutique fashion Shop called "La Casse". On the Monday morning Helen suggested that if I liked I could spend the day there with them. I readily agreed and before long found myself helping with the window dressing. The shop was in a fashionable part of Vancouver and most of the articles were of good quality and therefore expensive. I was on my feet all day and by the evening was quite worn out. Shop work made me very tired. Helen said there was a nice little restaurant nearby called The White Spot; we ordered Chicken in the Basket.

I worked in the shop all week and began to enjoy it, I made my first sale of a coat and skirt costing 110c$. Two hours latter in came a person who spoke French only. I took charge and to my great delight made a sale of a gaily coloured jacket for 85c$ - "my feet were killing me", I wrote in my diary. Again, dined at The White Spot. I continued to work there to help Helen and to repay her for all her kindness. More window dressing and sorting new stock. I enjoyed this and tried on many outfits that I fancied. During the weekend I met Helens friend Marjorie and had tea at the Marine Room at Eatons, a very smart department store, it cost a fortune! Marjorie then took me on to some friends at Forest Hills where they looked at slides of B.C. and Nova Scotia; very beautiful.

Tuesday 7th September I stayed home all day catching up on my letter writing - especially about Income tax and my National Insurance. Next day in the Shop I sold nothing, Oh dear! Feet not so bad, but the following day I was lucky enough to sell a coat and skirt for cash - 110c$.

On Friday I received a cable from Mrs Chaplin in Vevey Switzerland saying "WE NEED YOU. COME BACK SOON". Glory be! She must be desperate. What should I do? I had not finished my planned holiday. I cabled back saying "REGRET IMPOSSIBLE. WILL WRITE". This I did, saying that it was impossible to cancel my arrangements that had taken so long to prepare. I would, however try to shorten my stay as much as possible.

Many years latter my friends and family in England were rather surprised that I took this attitude. I had the best job I had had so far, would I not prejudice my relationship with the Chaplin's if I refused to go back quite soon? During my whole life so far I had done everything as I wanted and I found it difficult to understand other people's point of view. In spite of my religious upbringing other people thought I was self-righteous, to a degree.

I continued my vacation with a clear conscience. Working in the shop I could forget my other responsibilities. I enjoyed making sales and always totalled them up at the end of the day. One incident occurred while I was working in the shop which probable demonstrates why I did not involve myself in any male relationship. A Chinese couple came in and selected a c$389 outfit but while doing so the lady tripped and fell down two steps. I was able render first-aid and apparently no damage was done. The husband however, began to criticise the staff and said that the outfit was grossly overpriced and demanded a reduction. Whatever the outcome, the couple left with their purchases. My comment was, "I hate men". Was my attitude coloured by my experience with my father? I shall never know, but all my life I tended to criticise men generally.

On Sundays I always went to communion and afterwards to lunch with someone or other. My diary records visiting friends almost every evening or going to a show or a recital. A movie, "The Desert Rats"; Danny Kaye in "Knock on Wood". One Saturday I visited the navel Aircraft Carrier "Canadien".

October came and went with the same routine, but on November 12th a letter came from KK saying: Please. Please. Please. Come back. We all want you back.

This was the first anniversary of the day that I had first step foot into the Manoir. The Chaplin's had offered to pay my airfare home to Geneva. Now what should I do? I really had no reason to refuse. Two days latter I went to United Airlines and bought a ticket home. I wrote to KK to say I would be home on January 2nd 1955. On December 1st, my birthday, a grand party took place. Everyone came that I had made friends with in Vancouver. I was 48 years old.

As planned when I arrived at the Manoir after being picked up in Geneva airport by George the chauffeur, KK welcomed me with open arms. Thank God you've come! We have so much to do, with Mr and Mrs Chaplin constantly going off to London in connection with his new film "A King in New York" we have been told to take the children away on holiday as much as possible during the summer. In the meantime we are to get back to our usual routine that worked so well.

Mrs Chaplin has recently given up her American citizenship in protest at Mr Chaplin's treatment during the communist purges instigated by Senator McCarthy. She now became a full British citizen. The children appeared to be pleased to have me back. They had grown during the last six months and Geraldine, at 11 years old, was becoming a regular young lady. Brother Michael had nearly caught her up for height. Both of these were now going to the senior school in Lausanne. Jose and Vicky were still at the local school in Corsier.

My duties now reverted to the usual routine of taking them to school and bringing them home; seeing that they were properly dressed and helping with homework every evening. Shopping trips to Lausanne were always popular, when the children wanted something quite unsuitable, I had to dissuade them to buy something different. These trips always ended with ice creams and cream buns at a restaurant down by the lake at Ouchy where the Lake Steamers came in. Here they could feed the swans and ducks and I could sit and enjoy the sun while they played.

Great excitement during Easter. An invitation was received to attend the Wedding of my friend Francoise who was marrying Jean Vallet. Would the two girls Josey and Vicky be bridesmaids? Mrs Chaplin agreed, and dressmaking went ahead. On the 25th September the wedding took place with me seeing that the two girls did their duties.

Celebrities continued to visit the Manoir. Mr Jerry Epstein was almost now part of the family; he had been staying for several months helping Mr Chaplin with his new film. Every day working in his study they would try out new situations and gags, together with composing the music. These were trying times for KK and myself. The children at all times must be kept out of the way and above all quiet, no going near Mr Chaplin's study.

Eventually everything was ready for shooting the film and all the family, including KK and myself, moved to London staying as usual at the Savoy Hotel. Geraldine, Michael, Josie and Vicky together with baby Eugene were occupying rooms adjacent to their parents. I was in charge of the eldest and planned a conducted tour of London. This went down extremely well but before long they were looking for more interesting things to do, simple things that children most enjoy. Pinnie suggested they moved to the seaside, and soon a hotel at Eastbourne in Sussex was selected as suitable; right on the seafront. KK and I set off with all the children and commenced a week of bathing and building sand castles, Punch and Judy shows, donkey rides and a lot of ice cream. They thoroughly enjoyed themselves, out of the way of newsmen and cameras.

I knew that Eastbourne was only a short way along the coast from my cousins in Hampshire and resolved to visit them. I left KK in Eastbourne with Geraldine, Michael and Vicky and set off with Josie by train to Fareham where I was met by Rose, who took us home to their farm. Josie was entranced by this interlude, where she was to sleep in a small beamed bedroom with uneven floorboards. On the farm were cows, calves of all ages and chicken. Ken, Roses son, was at that time in charge of the cows and calves and Josie went with him across the fields to fetch the herd in for milking. She thought this was fun and she was able to stroke many of the more docile cows. Tea round a huge table with the family was unusual for her, as when at home in Switzerland the children eat in their own dining room downstairs at the rear of the house on the ground floor.

Two days later, back to Eastbourne, where they spent another week before returning to the Savoy.

Things were not going as planned for the film. Mr Chaplin could not get used to the way English film studios did their work, quite different to the ones in California. Tea at 4 o'clock always annoyed him, such a waste of time. Mr and Mrs Chaplin decided that they should move to a more secluded hotel. Great Fosters Hotel in Surrey was chosen as this was near Shepperton Studios where the film was being shot. It was a huge Elizabethan Mansion with beautiful gardens. It was at this point that Michael was due to appear in the film as a ragamuffin, I had been instructed not to allow his hair to be cut for several months beforehand. He certainly looked scruffy. I had been helping him to rehearse his lines and was confident he would be OK. The time came for his debut in films and a whole week was spent perfecting the shots. Mr Chaplin was never satisfied and demanded another shoot. Eventually they said that they were satisfied with the rushes, and Michael could relax. The following day I took Michael out to the nearest hairdresser for a short trim. Now that looks better I said and returned to the Hotel.

Just before breakfast the next day Mr Chaplin came in to say he had looked at the rushes again and had decided to take another shot. "Glory be"! I exclaimed, What should I do? At that moment Michael came along and I told him that another shoot would be required. Michael thought this was great fun and opened Mr Chaplin's door just a little to see if he was working; I am going in to see if he notices, he said. He went in and stayed a few minutes and presently came out to say he did not even look at me. There was nothing for it but to tell Mr Chaplin what I had done. I saw my job vanishing in thin air. Later in the morning I knocked on his door and went in and told him what I had done, he began to laugh and laugh and said don't upset yourself we will put a wig on him.

Eventually the filming came to an end and we all moved back to the Manoir. The family was able to get back into their old routines. It has been said that Mrs Chaplin did not spent much time with her children but I thought this was unfair as she was completely attached to her husband and he, being 36 years older, required that little bit more attention. She always, without fail, after they had eaten at night came to their rooms to kiss them goodnight and read the youngest a story.

Mrs Chaplin had a regular visit by her friend who was a physiotherapist. The treatment, she said, did her good and she always felt much better afterwards. Her name was Elfie who lived with her mother in a rather grand chalet in the village of St Legier quite near Corsier. Elfie also owned a small apartment nearby which I used to use during my days off from the Manoir. Also I arranged to rent it for a short while so that my cousins Audrey and Ken from England could stay there during their holidays. Elfie's mother had been married to a clergyman who had at some time been the chaplain to the Emperor Haile Selassie of Ethiopia. They were also the family that owned the Chalet at Crans Montana where the Chaplin family always went for their winter sports.

Time seemed to pass by very quickly and for the next three years I was always busy with the children. The older they got the more attention they required. I was however able to take a holiday in this period. I went to Beirut, visiting the Moslem Quarter, then on to Jordan and Israel. My diaries say I visited Jerusalem, Via Dolorossa, Calvary Site, Garden of Gethsemane and Bethlehem. Also the River Jordan where John the Baptist was baptised. I managed to get several good photographs of these areas. I was heavily influenced by the ambience of these places; it strengthened my religious beliefs that "God would always provide and look after me". Indeed, it appeared to be true, I was in a very lucky position. I was housed, fed and salaried. I had no outgoings, only clothes; my bank balance looked quite healthy.

It was always very difficult to understand that when I visited the UK why my relations did not travel more often. They said they had mortgages or rents and rates and taxes, running a car and many other expenses. They simply could not afford it. I should count my blessings, which in funny sort of way I did.

It is interesting to read Pinnies diaries to find out exactly what her average week entailed:-

SUNDAY.

Dull day. Children will not get dressed, Josie with sore throat, made her take medicine. Mr and Mrs C want them all ready to go with them by car to friends for lunch. Went to communion at Vevey, afterwards to lunch with Ann Hodgeson and family [friends] at the "Chateau Restaurant". Nice food.

MONDAY.

Sunny. Josie still had soar throat. Collected Mary the cook from town after taking kids to school. Music lessons for Josie. Geraldine to ballet lessons. Auntie Gypsy to lunch. Hair permed 38sf. KK treated me to dinner at Chez Pierre, frogs legs with asparagus. Bed at 11.00 p.m.

TUESDAY.

Sunny. Lunch at Frankies. Made brownie cakes, children with runny noses. Homework not completed. Dinner, Beef Strogonoff. Mr Chaplin's early films in evening. Whiskey before bed.

WEDNESDAY.

Overcast. Went up to Crans after breakfast with Alfie [friend]. Had lunch at hotel, nice. Delighted to see Frankie. Lemon cake for tea. All homework completed. Vickie playing up.

THURSDAY.

Glorious day. All family invited to the famous Swiss Circus. "Knie" in town at Vevey. KK and me were included. Ringside seats. Took Rolls car, Mrs C had all the tickets. "Glory Be" when we arrived we were one short. I had to give way! WAS I MAD. Mr Chaplin was greeted with loud applause when they took their seats. He fed buns to the elephants. Went to local hotel for a stiff drink.

FRIDAY.

Rabbits got out and disappeared. Spent all morning looking for them. Commotion in bird cage, it was the rabbits. Drat them!!. Made kissing cakes. All children home for weekend.

SATURDAY.

Shopping in Vevey. Shirts for the boys. Underwear for the girls. Walked the promenade with the kids. Ice creams all round. News from Canada. Bank of Montreal wrote to say I had been awarded a monthly pension of C$ 115.44 when I reach my 60th birthday. Not much but it will all help.

Pinnie could never rest for long, she was always planning something for the future. Even on a weekly basis she visited friends and attended films and theatres, dined and wined at the most luxurious establishments whenever she could find time. What other employer would enable their staff to combine such a personal lifestyle with their contractual responsibilities?

Time went by with me working roughly the same pattern. 1957 saw another increase in the Chaplin family. A girl, Jane was born. The fourth daughter. As usual KK was in charge. But this meant that I was in charge of one more child. Geraldine 13, Michael 11, Josie 8, Vickie 6 and Eugene [Tad] 4.

Mrs Chaplin suggested that as they were so busy with filming etc. the nannies should take the children away to a nice warm place during the summer. Jamaica was chosen and all the arrangements made. We were to stay at the house of Mr Chaplin's old friends, Mr and Mrs Spence. A lovely house called "High Hope" at St Annes Bay. It was a beautiful location, high up overlooking the sea. A large swimming pool was enjoyed by everyone. Mr Chaplin had arranged a personal guard called Winston for the children who came with us everywhere. No chances were taken; there was always the risk of abduction leading to demands for ransom etc. The visit coincided with the third anniversary of Jamaican independence and great gatherings of the population took place. The children joined in, in Nassau the capital there was fancy dress parades and West Indian music parties everywhere. Mr Sidney Chaplin arrived with his wife Noelle and their son, Stephan. This was a very pleasant interlude. Warm and sunny everyday.

We returned to Vevey at the end of August and KK went off on her annual holiday to Scotland. With the help of a nurse I was now in sole charge. Baby Jane was no trouble but there was no time for my usual visits to friends; I was tied to the Manoir most of the time. I found this very constricting but managed in my usual fashion of never being beaten. However, I was glad when KK got back.

September came and with it the start of school term. The eldest two were still at Lausanne all the week and the other three at the local school in Corsier. Homework every night, in bed by eight after going to see mother and father in the sitting room.

Sometimes Mr Chaplin would start playing a game with them. Monopoly or Draughts. This meant they would be able to stay up late. Mrs Chaplin, during these intimate moments with her children, showed great love and quiet affection. Although she was much younger than him, she had created a home of great serenity, and her husband reacted to this. In the peace of her home she quietly exerts her own influence over his work. He called her his literary brain, she was always telling him something was wrong in his scripts, she always made him put it right. He always said that with Oona to look after me, and my children to inspire my work, nothing can hurt me. She is the salt of the earth.

Celebrities came and went at the Manoir, including Mr Sidney Chaplin and his current girlfriend, Miss Judy Holliday. Rex Harrison and Kay Kendall came to stay for a few days. I was able to talk with them when they were in the garden with the children. It was quite exciting and I was able to get most of their autographs for my collection.

Time seemed to roll by quickly. I was so busy with the children that I hardly had time to take a personal holiday.

I always took a deep interest in each of the children. They came to me for advice and sometimes vented their anger on me for refusing something. Each one of them had a different personality, which meant that I treated one differently from another. I really became very close to them but was always aware that I should at no time try to replace their mother.

As we have already seen, Jane was born in 1957, but two years later, low and behold, another child was born, Annette. This made seven, the family was now so large that more staff were required at the Manoir. We had George the chauffeur and an assistant, Gino the butler, Yvonne the housemaid [she cleaned all the shoes], Mary the cook and her assistant, Walter and two other gardeners who looked after the large garden and a very large greenhouse, supplying most of the salads, vegetables and flowers for the house. At the peak we were 12 in number.

In the summer of 1960 it was decided that we should take the children for a holiday to Southern Ireland. This turned out to be a great success. We rented a cottage in the extreme southwest called Reenroe, entirely on its own near a beautiful bay. I recall it belonged to Mike and Mrs Moriarty, who arranged horse riding and salmon fishing. The children were able to run wild over the dunes and hillsides, watching the locals digging peat and making friends with their children. No sign of the press or photographers. Just me with my camera. We were to return to this ideal spot many times in the future.

Returning to the Manoir, life for me was the same as usual. But with increased staff I was able to reactivate my social life with friends. It was becoming increasingly regular that Mrs Chaplin would forget when it was my day off and would ring for me to do various things on that day. This secretly annoyed me and I looked for some method of avoiding this.

One friend I had met in Vevey, while at church, was another Englishwoman named Anne Hodgeson. Anne was a divorcee, living in a small flat on the waterfront. She was in the process of building a chalet in the beautiful hamlet of Les Avant. The home was in two parts, upstairs flat and downstairs flat. It overlooked the Rocher de Nay mountain and Montreux. I helped her with the planning and furniture. The upstairs flat would be let to pay for the bank loan for building. The bottom flat was available for Anne and any of her personal friends who required it. I thought this might be an answer to my problem, I could leave the Manoir on the evening of my conge and be in Les Avant all next day without interference. This I arranged and it worked very well. Anne and I remained good friends for the rest of her life.

CHAPTER ELEVEN

Christopher James was born on July 8th 1962. This was to be the last child, bringing the total to eight. Now we were a huge family and my responsibilities increased accordingly. Geraldine 18, Michael 16, Josie 13, Vickie 11, Eugene 9, Jane 5 and Annie 3.

Geraldine and Michael more or less looked after themselves, but at all times there were always at least 4 children with me. It was essential now to organise many outings and visits to keep the children occupied and interested; holidays abroad were always welcomed.

Mr and Mrs Chaplin were regularly in London working on his Chaplin Review films and writing his biography, therefore out of term time KK and I were in sole charge. Apart from Miss Ford, who was Mr Chaplin's personal secretary, with offices in Paris, looking after his film interests worldwide, she was a law unto herself. She was very self assured, I am sure she ruled those offices with a rod of iron. It was rumoured that she worked for Sir Winston Churchill during the war. Good training I thought.

During the whole summer we had a continuous set of Birthday Parties in the garden. Local school children were invited, organising games and supervising swimming in the pool. Mary providing the cakes and sandwiches.

Lets go to Eastbourne again said Eugene; Oh lets, chorused the others. We want the seaside. Accordingly we made arrangements at the same Hotel we had been before and we all set off to London Airport. By train to Eastbourne. As well as the usual amusements we decided to visit many other places of interest. Pevensey Castle and Beachy Head. We stayed for two weeks and returned home in late August.

Mr and Mrs Chaplin had by now returned from London. The children were off to school and KK took her annual leave to Scotland. When she returned it gave me some time to visit all my local friends and spending a few days up at Les Avant with Anne Hodgeson. She had called her chalet "Chalet Herrison", meaning hedgehog.

Winter was approaching fast and the thought of winter sports at Crans Montana made me book up the usual hotels but fortunately our good friend Frankie, who you will remember lived near Vevey, offered her family Chalet almost in the centre of the town. This was superb, we all arranged to go after Christmas was over. In the meantime we all went shopping for presents. The boys would not come with the girls and visa versa. They wanted their choice of presents to remain secret. Late December we decorated the tree and the main rooms of the house, wrapped the presents and made Advent calendars.

The two eldest girls were growing up really fast. They were teenagers and becoming interested in boys. I was told to keep a very watchful eye on them. Josie was very secretive about who she had met at parties and while at school in Lausanne. I found out that she had been meeting a certain boy after school; should I tell her parents? I decided to have a good talk to her and made her promise not to do it again.

Christmas came and we all looked forward to a family lunch together, Kay Kay and I included, also Auntie Gypsy from Lausanne. Another relation came for Christmas - I had not met this one before. She was Betty Tetrick, Mr Chaplin's cousin from London, a widow who took a great interest in the children. The table was decorated in red with two candle displays. Traditional crackers were in abundance, supplying the paper hats and small toys and puzzles. It was lovely. Mary had excelled herself with all the traditional foods common in England, even sixpences hidden in the Christmas Puddings. The meal lasted all afternoon until Mr Chaplin went off for a rest but, in the evening, he insisted that we all went to the Movie viewing room to see "The Gold Rush". Not again, said the children, but reluctantly went.

1963 came in with another late night party; fireworks on the lawn in the snow; hot sausages afterwards.

Geraldine, the eldest, has now become a lively young woman. A bit of a tomboy and the image of her mother. She likes to go to Dances and all other forms of entertainment. She is very aware of her slim figure and always dressed accordingly. She was very fond of her little black dress and would always wear it when she could not decide on anything else. We would scour the shops looking for suitable dresses in Lausanne. She would use her mother's gloves to match the dresses and also some of my costume jewellery. She was very aware of who she was and would pose for photographers if they were present. She has dreams of becoming a ballet dancer and would sometimes perform for us in the drawing room. Mother, however insisted that she complete her Matrix examinations first.

Mid January we all set off for Crans, boarding the train at Vevey and going as far as Sierre in the Rhone valley and then by funicular up to Crans. It was only a short walk to the Chalet Les Vezzaches where we established ourselves, the children rushing from room to room choosing which bedroom for themselves. Mr and Mrs Chaplin came latter on by car.

The snow was deep and all the branches of the trees heavy with snow, it was a very beautiful scene. All the children, except baby Christopher of course, were out early playing in the garden. Every day we went up the ski lifts, sometimes to the very top where we slowly skied down to the bottom of the run. KK and I were terrified they would injure themselves, we had to keep a tight reign on them. But all went well and by the end of a week the novelty had worn off. We had to look for alternative amusement, skating at Montana on the public rink was the answer and we went there every day.

At the end of most days all the family went out to a restaurant for dinner; we were very lucky as when the owners saw who we were gave us a prime table and ensured we had good service. Unfortunately Mr Chaplin caught a heavy cold, and was confined to bed for a few days, Mrs Chaplin in constant attendance.

Two weeks at Crans was enough and we all returned to the Manoir. It could not come soon enough for Mr Chaplin who disliked the cold. The children were due back at school and the household returned to normal. Mr Chaplin was finishing his autobiography so that we saw little of him. He was confined to his very pleasant study on the ground floor where he worked for hours at a time and we had to keep the children clear of his window. During this time many celebrities visited the Manoir, most in connection with a proposed new film that he was planning. It was to be called "A Countess from Hong Kong" starring his son Sidney, Marlon Brando, Sophia Loren, Partick Cargill and Margaret Rutherford.

When Mr Chaplin's autobiography was published in 1964, Mr and Mrs Chaplin and Josie went on a publicity tour to Sweden leaving KK and I in charge. The household continued as usual during the year. There were no major changes and when during July Mrs Chaplin suggested I should take some time off I was delighted and arranged to visit my relatives in England. A phone call to Nottingham revealed that Phil had bought a new car, an Austin Cambridge, would I like to come with them to Southern Ireland for a few days? I readily agreed and made plans accordingly. I flew to London and on to Nottingham by train. We set off for Fishguard in south Wales and crossed by ferry to Eire at Rosslare, We toured the south coast as far as Cork, stayed for two days and continued on to the extreme south west, Bantry, Dingle. Kenmare bays were the most beautiful I had seen, to stand and watch the sun go down in the west, with the light turning from bright sunshine to reds and golds until it was dark. Then returning to our hotel in Kenmare where we dined off freshly caught Salmon and finishing the evening with a tot of Irish whiskey. Superb.

The next day we toured the lakes of Killarney, Birr Castle, Cong and Croagh. Patrick finishing up at Ashford Castle Hotel, the ancestral home of the Guinness brewing family. Cousin Phil was a pleasant companion but I thought him a confirmed bachelor. The holiday finished all too soon and back to the Manoir I went.

It had become the usual practice that when KK and I celebrated our birthdays we would go to Frankie's house for a party. Frankie had by this time produced a daughter named Sabine and we were asked to bring along the youngest of our charges for her company. These were always a cross between a children's party and grown ups party, but we all enjoyed it. These were memorable occasions. Frankie would always bake a cake with one candle representing each decade.

Time flew by and before long it was 1967. Mr Chaplin was well on the way to finishing his new film and had arranged a press meeting in London on Monday November 4th to announce his plans. Geraldine and Josie were to go as well. They all stayed as usual at the Savoy Hotel. Geraldine was now 23 years old and very beautiful. Josie was 18 and longing to be in the centre of the theatre world. The world press turned up at this meeting. Sophia Loren at her most alluring took most of the attention but the two Chaplin girls were photographed almost as much. Mr Chaplin announced his intention to begin filming shortly. Was this to be his last film? You wait and see said Mr C.

Life at the Manoir continued to be rather hectic. Mr and Mrs Chaplin were busy travelling to Paris, London and other places connected with his new film. The year seemed to pass very quickly. Two occasions dominated this period, first it was the 80th birthday of Mr Chaplin and secondly the marriage of Josie. Both meant that I would be required to do my share of the arrangements, especially regarding the children.

April 16th 1969 was Mr Chaplin's 80th Birthday, a grand family luncheon was planned and everyone was expected to be there. I lectured the eldest to be understanding towards their father and to make sure they presented themselves appropriately dressed together with a present. KK and I made sure the youngest ones did not let the side down. Everyone arrived on time and the party commenced. Mary, in the kitchen, excelled herself again providing four courses together with two types of Swiss wine.

Presents and congratulatory cards arrived from all over the world. We all sung "Happy birthday to you". After the meal we all took photographs. It was a very happy day indeed.

Josie had been seeing a young man whom she had met at a party in Geneva. He was the son of a Greek furrier who had a business and shop in the centre of the town. It was the kind of shop that if you had to inquire the price of the coats displayed in the windows you could not afford them.

His name was Nicholas Sistovaris; Nicky to all of us. He was in partnership with his brother and father in the business. The relationship flourished and in due course Nicky asked Mr Chaplin for Josie`s hand in marriage. During the course of the arrangements for the wedding the Sistovaris family visited the Manoir to finalise the details. During these visits I became quite friendly with them. Mr and Mrs Sistovaris were very charming and invited me to their shop in Geneva when I was in town. He told her that they went to Moscow to buy the furs and made them up to order in Geneva.

The date set for the wedding was the 21st June 1969. After the marriage there was to be a grand reception at the Manoir; blue and white striped marquis in honour of the Greek national flag were erected in the garden to house all the guests. The big day arrived and everyone was up early. We all had a light breakfast and then KK and I set about dressing the smaller children for the occasion. They were all agog, this was the first family wedding and we new nothing must go wrong. Guests began to arrive from all over the world, many from as far away as California.

The local Gendarmerie had provided a police presence to control not only the traffic but the many press reporters and cameramen thronging the road outside asking to be allowed in for photographs. After the ceremony everyone came back to the Manoir for the reception.

I stuck to my motto of "Nothing for the dumb" and mixed with the guests while keeping an eye on the children. I met many celebrities from the film world together with the Chaplin family friends from England and locally. It was a memorable day for all of them. The press had a field day and pictures of the happy couple appeared in newspapers all over the world.

In between these events I went about my duties with the children, taking them shopping and to other events that they were interested in. It was not unusual that when I had to go down to Vevey on various errands, I took the youngest with me. One of my prime delights was to walk the promenade along the waterfront from Montreux, Clarens, La Tour de Peilz, Vevey and on to St Saphorin. The children came with me and enjoyed playing in the communal play areas and looking for fish among the small rocks along the way. This area, known as the Swiss Riviera enjoyed a microclimate that was not in any other part of Switzerland. The mountains on the north side of the Lake had sunlight all day from sunrise to sunset. The sunlight was reflected up from the water onto the hillsides making it ideal for grapes.

There is a saying that cleanliness is next to Godliness, if that is so then the people living in this area are very Godly. The paths are swept daily and the litterbins emptied every morning. The flowerbeds along the whole of the coast are always immaculate; never any weeds. The trees are pollarded annually to provide shade in the summer. This is the area that produces most of the wine consumed in Switzerland. The hillsides are covered with neat and tidy vines with places where you can taste the wine at your leisure. I would select a lakeside seat and enjoy the panorama of the High Alps opposite and the white paddle steamers plying the lake. Sometimes we would take a trip across the lake to Evian in France where after an ice cream would return by the next boat. These outings made my lifestyle very worthwhile. I knew that there were not many places that offered such a romantic setting. I was indeed lucky.

Life at the Manoir continued in the normal way. Every day there was someone leaving or coming to stay. Among the celebrities were Claire Bloom, Somerset Maughan, Arthur Rubenstein, Sophia Loren, Jerry Epstein, Sydney and Noelle Chaplin, Noel Coward, Jacqueline Kennedy, David Niven, Diana Cooper, and Auntie Gypsy. I was able to get the autographs of all these people.

Auntie Gipsy was Mr Chaplin's sister-in-law from London and had a permanent suite at the fabulous "Beau Rivage" Hotel in Laussanne. I used to visit her when I was in town. Many lesser well known people came to visit the Chaplin family as well as my personal friends who all signed my visitors book. The total came to over one hundred.

My passion for writing letters did not diminish as I got older. Letters to the British Royal Family went off whenever there was a wedding, birth or funeral in the family. When the Duchess of Kent died in 1968 I wrote to express my condolences to her daughter. A reply was received as follows-

THATCHED HOUSE LODGE.

RICHMOND PARK.

SURREY.

September 26TH 1968.

Dear Madame Pyniger.

Princess Alexandra was deeply touched by your thought in writing to her at this time.

Her Royal Highness would like you to know how much she appreciated your kindness.

Yours Sincerely

Mary Fitzalan Howard.

Lady in Waiting.

It was now seventeen years since I first started working for the Chaplin family. During that time I had found so many friends that it was quite impossible to keep up my contacts with all of them. The ones living locally in the Vevey area were the ones I saw most, particularly the ones that I met most weeks at Church. We had quite unintentionally formed a habit of meeting for a cup of tea and cakes at the Hotel Famille that was situated next to the main railway station. This Hotel was originally started to cater for Christians travelling through Vevey en-route to various centres of pilgrimage. They provided reasonable priced accommodation and food for everyone.

The establishment was currently in the hands of the Krahenbuhl family and I was pleased to have as a friend Madame Krahenbuhl who was delighted to have us all there for our almost weekly meetings. These were lovely interludes to our busy weekly routines. We were all invited to Madame Krahenbuhls daughter Susannes wedding on the 6th October to Gerard. The reception was held of course at the Hotel.

Another wedding that I was invited to was the marriage in Geneva of Johnny Sistovaris and Maria; Johnny was the brother of Nicky who had married Jose.

The third wedding that I was not lucky enough to be present was the marriage of my dear forth child Victoria who had been studying dance, ballet and music in Geneva and latterly in London. There she met Jean Baptiste Thierree who was born in Paris and started his working life in a circus and later joined the theatre as an actor. He subsequently directed many music hall shows. After returning to the circus he met Vicky and they both found that they were interested in the same things. Both of them worked together for some time, realising that the traditional circus with many animals had probably seen the best of its days, they began to work on a format that dispensed with animals but left the scenes to the imagination. Between them they created the "Le Cirque imaginaire". Their first production was at the Bloomsbury Theatre, London and later moved to the Whitehall Theatre. Patrons had to attend this production with an open mind to appreciate its success that indeed it was.

The couple were married on the 15th May, 1971 and it was not until several months later that they were able to visit us at the Manoir. I liked Jean very much and was sure their marriage would be a success. They had two children, Aurelia and James.

The next surprise for me was an official envelope arriving for me from London. Containing another invitation from the Lord Chamberlains office, who had been commanded by Her Majesty to invite me to an Afternoon Party in the Garden of Buckingham Palace on Wednesday, 21st July 1971 from 4 to 6 p.m.

When I mentioned my invitation to Mrs Chaplin she said that it was a coincidence that they would be in London themselves about this date. Come with us and the children who were still at home, go to the Palace and take a few days holiday afterwards. Glory be !!!. How lucky I was.

On 14th July we all arrived at the Savoy in London. That night St Paul's Cathedral staged a "Son et Lumier" and we all took a taxi to see it. The next day we visited Fortnum and Masons for tea and cakes; this brought back many memories of my earlier life in London. We also took in The Royal Academy and went to the theatre to see Henry James in the "The High Bid".

The Garden Party was a success as usual. I met many Canadians who were over here on holiday. The Royal Couple came quite near us but not near enough to speak to.

The following day I left the family and went on my way down south to my cousins in Hampshire. I stayed a few days on the farm where I was concerned about the health of Sidney, Roses husband. He was receiving treatment from his doctor for cancer. Hospitalisation was imminent.

I took off by coach to Bournemouth staying at the St Georges Hotel, visited Blandford, Canford Cliffs, Salisbury and Tollard Royal.

Back at Vevey on the 31st July. KK and I had plenty to do with the children who were all on holiday from school. Great news from Vicky, she had given birth to a Daughter at Montpellier in France on the 24th August and would be coming to stay soon.

My diaries now listed many of the usual activities I was doing from September onwards. Josie came with her son young Charlie, now nicknamed Charlie Bubbles, because of his high temperament and zest for life, never still, always bubbling. They all had tea out by the pool.

On 23rd I took the three youngest children to Bordighera, a seaside town just inside Italy on the Mediterranean Ligurian coast. Here we stayed at the Pension Manesal with a balcony looking out to sea. The weather was good so we bathed three times daily. Visited Mentone, Roquebrune [with a statue to Winston Churchill] and Monte Carlo. Returned to Vevey via Turin, Aosta and Martigne.

Letter waiting for me from cousin Rose in England. Husband Sidney admitted to the London Masonic Hospital; bad news indeed. I was getting problems with my teeth and a visit to the dentist resulted in four fillings and a new plate.

Gloria Vanderbilt, a friend of the Chaplin's, arrived. Much preparation and fuss but I got her Signature in my autograph book.

Sunday 14th was Remembrance Day in Vevey. The Church was packed and I met many of my friends afterwards. Had lunch at Hotel Famille. The post on Monday brought the news I had been expecting for some time, Roses husband Sydney had died. The funeral service was to be held on the 19th. I could not get away and sent a letter to Rose together with a wreath and a donation to cancer research.

I had asked Sidney some time previously to act as an executor for my estate when the time came. Now of course I had to find another. My relationship with Audrey and Ken, Sidney's son and daughter in law had progressed to such an extent that I had no problems in asking Ken if he would now take over from his father. He agreed and it was duly recorded in my will. Audrey and Ken never missed a visit to Vevey from that time onwards.

December 1st was my 65th birthday. Lots of cards, flowers and presents from all over the world, plus a cheque from Mrs Chaplin for 500sf. I was overcome. After a party Frankie showed me her new flat she had bought at St Legier. It was quite small but I could use it at any time.

Christmas was now nearly upon us and I did my usual bit of shopping with the children; my top floor flat was the dump for hiding the presents - the smell of perfume was overpowering. The 25th was devoted of course to the family, all round the large table for lunch and afterwards unwrapping the presents, Madame Astor and Mr Sistovaris were our guests and in the evening Mr Chaplin insisted we viewed his film "Limelight".

CHAPTER TWELVE

After my 65th birthday it seemed to me that I had started on a new period of my life. For the last five years I had been receiving payments accruing from my various pension schemes in Canada, England and Switzerland. The Canadian and Swiss pensions were paid into my local bank but my English pension was paid into my account at a Bank in London. This was used when I visited the U.K. I was reasonably satisfied that, come what may, I should be able to support myself in my old age. Whether I should stay in Switzerland or return to the U.K. I left in the hands of God.

Mr and Mrs Chaplin had never mentioned that I should retire and therefore life at the Manoir went on as usual. Once when I was in Geneva for two days with my Irish friend Carmel McGreevy, who worked at the United Nations, we went to a beautiful film, set in Southern Ireland during the struggle for independence. It was called "Ryan's Daughter", a tear jerking love story depicting the problems of the day.

Late January I lost my dear friend Gweneth, after a long illness. I had known her for several years; she was one of my circle of friends who lunched regularly each week with me at the Hotel Famille. Poor darling, now at peace.

The eldest of the family set off for London for the grand premier of the new film, "A Countess from Hong Kong". All the movie stars and paparazzi were out in force. Mr and Mrs Chaplin in the spotlight with Nicky Sistovaris and Josie as their guests. Nicky phoned home the next day to say the newspapers did not give it a good write up. Mr Chaplin was not amused. In fact when Mr Chaplin got home we had to send for Dr Perris to give him something to calm him down. A week later they were off again to Milan, for another Premier, this time much better. Afterwards we journeyed on to Rome where Mr Chaplin received an Italian Film Award. Unfortunately two of the children caught mumps and I had to fly back with them to Switzerland quickly. No small plane was available but somehow the Popes Private Jet was. What an honour. How this was arranged I shall never know.

Vickie at last arrived to show us her children. She now had two, a boy and a girl. They were great, just like their mother. Auntie Gipsy arrived to see them as well.

On the 28th March we left Vevey with Nicky, KK, Jane, Annie and Chris to have a few days holiday in Bermuda. On arrival at Geneva airport we were delayed by police and armed guards for two hours while they escorted the brother of King Hussein of Jordan on to his plane. It took us seven hours to arrive in Bermuda with travel officials not very kind. However the short holiday was a great success with a boat called the "Sea Venturer" taking us to various offshore islands.

Early June I watched the Funeral of the Duke of Windsor on T.V. I was touched and could not make up my mind if he would have made a good king. I decided to write to the Queen expressing my sadness and ensuring her of my continuing support during this period of reconciliation.

July 8th was Christopher's birthday. He was 10 years old and I still treated him as the baby. We had a great party around the pool with his school friends.

It was now time for my annual trip to the U.K. I booked a seat which turned out to be no 13; Glory be!. Arriving in Edinburgh I was met by George and Ester, my friends from London days. I stayed for 5 days and then off to London. Tea at Fortnum and Masons, of course. I took in a show and then off to Oxford where I visited the Ashmoleum Museum that was very busy, New College and the church of St Michaels. Spent some time at mother's grave, planted bulbs and said my prayers. Then off to lunch at the George and Dragon Pub at Wargrave on the river Thames.

By coach now to Hampshire. Staying with Rose at her bungalow in the pretty village of Meonstoke. Had tea with friends Francis Wheatley and Mrs Cobb. Visited cousins Joan and Andy with their two daughters. Church on Sunday at St Andrews, Meonstoke. Afterwards to Audrey and Kens for tea. Leaving a copy of my Will with him. Audrey, who was a Hospital Administrator in Southampton, was able to get a few days off and the two of us set off in her car for Bournemouth; the St Georges Hotel. There, the rear garden faces the sea and during the afternoons we would sit in the sun discussing our lives. Audrey was a good listener and I asked her why she waited hand and foot upon her husband Ken as well as holding down a job? She took some time to answer and then she asked me if I had ever been in love? She went on to explain that before her marriage her mother had said to her that she should read and digest the marriage vows that she would take before Almighty God, never be jealous of other people even if they appeared to be better off than her. She had tried to do these things and thought that her mothers advice was sound. Both her and Ken shared everything, she was confident that he was just as much in love with her as she with him.

She suggested that as I had never been in that position I could never understand. It was true I never had, my finances were never shared, I never needed a house and I could always do as I liked with my life and now even in my job.

It was at this point that I was forced to make a confession. One day a few months previously I was making a rail journey and found I was sitting opposite an elderly gentleman who was reading a book. He took no notice of me as I sat down but after about half an hour he put the book down and I saw that it was a Bible. I could not help saying that I had noticed what book it was and reading it always gave me great courage to face the world. He turned out to be an Englishman from Hertfordshire. His name was Hartley Holmes. We talked a great deal during the journey and found we had a lot in common regarding religion. He said he had lost his wife and was missing her greatly and that he had two children now grown up and left home. At the end of my journey to Vevey he asked me if he could see me again, I hesitated but gave him my address. In due course he contacted me and came to Vevey staying at the Hotel Pavillon near the station. We met several times and got on very well. We wined and dined and discussed our respective lives. At the end of his stay he suggested we ought to consider marriage. This shook me rigid. At my age! And he was 7 years older. I said I must consider this very carefully and would write to him when I had made a decision.

All this I told to Audrey on that hot day in Bournemouth. What did she think? Audrey was amazed; she had always thought that I was a confirmed spinster. She analysed the situation, commenting that our ages ought to be taken into consideration, although at the moment he was active and healthy, it may not last and I would find myself looking after him, perhaps bedridden. And what would his family think? Would they accept another woman in their family? In any case I would have to move back to the U.K. All her friends were now in Switzerland. Her life would change dramatically. She intimated that it would not be a good move. She would regret it. I listened to her advice and thought I would leave it for another few days before I wrote to him again. In due course I wrote and explained to him my doubts about such a marriage. I received back a beautiful letter, saying how disappointed he was and asked if we could still be friends and meet from time to time. He sent me his love and the Bible he was reading when we first met.

I returned to Vevey to find that Charlie Bubbles, Christopher, Annette and Jane were all home for the summer holidays. In spite of Geraldine and Nicky living nearby in Corseaux, young Charlie spent most of his time at the Manoir. Mrs Chaplin said that Mr Sistovaris had invited any of the family to use his property in Greece for a holiday if they wished. It would now be a good time to go and see Greece for the first time.

Saturday August 5th 1972 saw us all up early to get to the airport. Our arrival in Greece was greeted with blue skies and sunny weather. Mr Sistovaris [senior] met us with his car to take us to his property in Galixidi, a lovely house overlooking the sea. Every day after breakfast at 8 we would set off to explore the local village of St. George in a motorboat. Lunchtime aperitifs of langoustines, goat's cheese, tomatoes with fresh olives, washed down with good red wine. Swimming after lunch every day. The evening meal was spent on the patio under a grapevine. Superb!

Mrs Sistovaris; who we were to call granny; was a lovely person. She adored children and young Charlie and another grandchild Katia were quite at home in her company. She was quiet and always peaceful. She very seldom came to Geneva preferring to stay in Greece, at home.

The holiday went by quickly. Everyday going somewhere different, accompanied by Mr Sistovaris. We visited Edipsos and Parnasus. Lunch with the family; we had spaghetti and fish with tomato salad, honey buns wrapped in foil. Then swimming, water skiing, learning Greek dancing. Annie gave an exhibition with a local young man at the end of the holiday.

All good things come to an end. At home the children went back to school and I went about my duties as usual. The Chaplin's were away in Paris so that we had the house to ourselves during the day. I took this opportunity to sort out all the unwanted baby clothes and was able to send to Audrey in the U.K. a large parcel of clothes suitable for her son, Julian who was a little younger than Eugene. This was, of course, was with the permission of Mrs Chaplin who was always extremely generous with left off items.

One day Mrs Chaplin came to see me in my room. She said that I had been using the car with the driver too much and would I please restrict my usage to affairs of the family and not to my personal use. I considered myself well and truly told off!

Quite out of the blue I received a message from Ken and Audrey in England that they would be visiting Vevey on their annual holiday and would like to see me. I arranged for them to stay at Frankies new flat at St Legier. They jumped at the idea. Ken and Audrey came to the Manoir, where I showed them around the house and garden. The pool was free so that we took the opportunity for a quick bathe but after about half an hour I looked up and saw Mr and Mrs Chaplin leaving the house and walking towards the pool; "Glory be", we very quickly collected our things and made ourselves scarce. Mr Chaplin hated meeting strangers and I would be accused of overreaching my position.

The following day they picked me up in their car. I wanted to show them the beautiful countryside around Vevey and eventually did a complete circumnavigation of Lake Leman, calling in to see Nicky and Mr Sistovaris in Geneva at their fur salon. We took tea at the Beau Rivage Hotel and then on to St Saphorin for dinner at 8.o'clock. It must have been a successful outing because they came back to the area on holiday for many years afterwards.

December 1st was my birthday. I received 14 cards and many phone calls wishing me well from local friends. It was my conge [day off] and I stayed in bed until 11.00 a.m. writing letters etc. then a quick bath and off to Lausanne for lunch with my friends there. Dinner that evening was at the Grappe D`or. My friend Alfie drove me home.

I was becoming increasingly concerned about my investments in De Beers Mines of South Africa. Since being in Switzerland I had made so many friends from Africa, both white and black and I had become very sympathetic with the South African black peoples struggle for emancipation. My investment did not help their cause. I decided to sell all my shares and reinvested in the U.K. with the Marks and Spencer Group. I always used them when in the U.K. and thought them good value for money.

A surprise awaited me one day just before Christmas when the Post brought me an official buff envelope from the U.K. It was from the U.K. Government repaying a war loan that I had made to them during my stay in London and Oxford. The cheque was for £3066.08. I hope it helped when they most needed it.

1973 opened with the usual skiing and winter sports at Crans Montana and Gstaad. The children coming and going. One day Josie came over to me and said, come with me. She took me across the room and introduced me to the Shah of Persia and his family whom she had became very friendly during our stay and received an invitation to visit them in their palace in Iran. He made arrangements for them to collect Visas for travelling from their embassy in Geneva.

Tad was in London at the Mermaid Theatre.

Young Charlie Bubble took a liking for bacon and eggs English style, he insisted I cooked for him whenever possible.

I still used the new flat at Les Avants for my conge; meeting Ann Hodgeson and friends and lunching at the nearby Hotel Hellioda.

I began to be alarmed about my legs and feet. All my life they had been in good health but lately I was experiencing great pain; varicose veins were a likely cause and I had tests to verify this. By March I could stand it no longer and arranged treatment by a specialist, Dr Karin Hertzog. What a relief!

April saw us all travelling to the South of France to the exclusive Cap Ferrat for a holiday. Much bathing at a private beach and eating at the most secluded restaurants. Saw John Mills and Lilly Palmer filming. Reporters and photographers followed us everywhere and were a jolly nuisance. On the following Sunday I went to the local Anglican Church for communion and returned to lunch where there were masses of Easter eggs for everyone.

We all returned to Vevey with Nicki, Jane and all the kids. On the 19th May it was Jane's birthday. Auntie Gypsy came and we all went to the zoo. These were memorable occasions as we seem to get on so well together. On the 31st I had my first row with KK. She seemed to think I had all the best jobs while she always stayed behind at home. Well, I could not let this go on so I apologised, saying I did not know she thought this way. Time healed our differences and all was well.

Back home with the usual routine. The days passed quietly except when Chris swallowed a 1 franc piece. Down to the doctors who said, Don't worry; nature will take its course.

I took the children to see David Niven in "Bridge Over the River Kwai". Excellent. He had called to see the Chaplin's recently as he lived quite near us at Chateau d'Oex. Other personalities who visited us were Maria Callas and Anthony Armstrong Jones who was very interested in my study of the British Royal Family.

I was due for a few days off so I decided to visit the U.K. I flew to Edinburgh and stayed with friends there. What a beautiful City!. The Forth bridge all lit up at night. What delicious food! From Scotland I took the train to Winchester where Rose met me and took me back to her bungalow in Meonstoke, Hampshire. We decided to take a few days on the Island of Jersey. Audrey, Ken's wife, took us to the Airport and we flew to St Helier staying at the Pomme D'Or Hotel. We toured the small Island, enjoying the delightful fresh crabs, caught locally. At the local theatre we saw The Harry Secombe Show. Very good. What at marvellous voice he has.

Returning to Meonstoke I visited most of my relations nearby. Before going up to London staying at the Commonwealth Club. There I was pleased to see Nennette from Belgium who was working as a trained nurse together with many of my old friends from London days.

Back in Vevey the family were all pursuing their individual lives, coming and going with hardly time to tell me about themselves. Chris was 11, Annie was 14 and Jane was 16 years old. There was only the youngest to worry about, Chris and Annie. They were not babies anymore; I realised my job was easy.

It was about this time that I had thoughts that this job would not last for ever. I contemplated that I might consider going to America, when during my luncheon session with my local friends, we invited a lady from the American embassy in Geneva. During our conversations she intimated that the Presidents wife, Jaqueline Kennedy was looking for a French speaking assistant Nannie to work in the "White House". Glory be! what an opportunity for someone. However, after I had more information I realised I was too old. But I did recommend another young lady for the post, who I believe was successful.

On 12th September Mr and Mrs Chaplin left for Paris. Betty Tetrick, Mr Chaplin's cousin, was staying with us at the time. The next morning she gave me a letter that she said was from Mrs Chaplin. It was indeed! I sat down and read it three times. It was, in fact, a letter terminating my employment. It was written in a very nice way. I suppose I could not be surprised as I said my job was coming to an end but I had not anticipated it just then.

The Letter:-

September 10th, 1973
MANOIR DE BAN
CORSIER SUR VEVEY

My dear Pinnie.

I`ve been wanting to talk to you about the future for some time, but keep postponing it because its difficult for me --- but the more I postpone it the more disagreeable I get as you probably notice. You brought up the subject yourself a few years ago and I admired you for doing it. Now it's my turn.

The time has inevitably come when there are really only two children, both over eleven, living at home. Sometimes I feel we are three women struggling over one small boy and I don't think its good for him and I don't think it brings out the best in me. Kay Kay is 70 and has been with us for 29 years---but you know all the reasons. You have been with me since Tad was a baby and now you've seen him announce his engagement. We've been through so much together that I don't want to write anything factual or breaking with the past.

But this year I must think ahead. We really will have to make a change and I'm sure you understand it. I mentioned a pension and I don't want to be vague about it: I will pay you 800 francs [Swiss] a month as long as I can, which I imagine will be for the rest of your life.

I suggest you continue to work here as before till the end of May. I want very much to talk to you about your future plans, whether you want to get another full-time job with children, which I'm sure would be very cosy [you would have a glowing reference from me] – whether you would like to live near here and do part time work --- whether you plan to retire. There are many possibilities. I hope we can find an arrangement where you are still close to the family, but of course, that's up to you.

I hate breaking the news. I've been putting it off for many months, ever since Jane moved downstairs, actually--- but with inflation and all that goes with it, the time has truly arrived.

With love as ever.

Oona C.

Well here it was. The situation that I had been expecting but never really thought it would come like this. I sat down to think it over. Surely Mrs Chaplin could have spoken to me personally, instead of sending me a letter. I went into KKs room to tell her. She had had a letter as well, but with her she was to be allowed to stay in the Manoir and do light duties. Her room was to be her home and the family would look after her in her latter years, come what may. She had been with them since their Californian days, so I supposed she deserved it. I had however, 9 months in which to arrange something else. Well, something will turn up I was sure. God willing.

In the afternoon Young Charlie arrived and with the two other kids went off to Vevey for a walk along the front, buying ice creams on the way. I looked at them more deeply than I had ever before. I should miss them and I hoped that when I told them, they would miss me. When we got home I went to my room to find a document that I had written several years previously when I was having tea with my friends in Vevey. We had decided to describe our work as we saw it and to let them read it, just as an exercise. I sat down to read it again and was satisfied that I would not change a word.

The Document:

The Family

Not dated. Believed to be, according to the text, about 1961.

There are seven reasons why no woman in her right mind would work for the Chaplin family: Geraldine, Michael, Josephine, Victoria, Eugene, Jane and Annette. Seven children with a spark of their fathers genius in their wide, over-innocent eyes, the girls with their mothers good looks — and maybe as strong headed? She did run away from her family as a teenager to marry a man in his fifties, didn`t she?

Mabel Pyniger, [Pinnie] a quiet smiling Canadian in her late forties, isn't of this opinion. She thinks her job of looking after the most famous children in the world undiluted fun.

The daughter of a Winnipeg deputy sheriff [Dirty water, yell the gang, gleefully translating Winnipegs Indian name] she makes only one concession to cold reality:

"If there are more to come", she admits "the house will have to split its sides".

This is always a possibility in a household where baby clothes and prams are never given away — but kept easily accessible for the next time.

Yet Charlie and Oona Chaplin live in a large 18th century mansion, the Manior de Ban, above Vevey, which they chose in 1952 when they arrived in Switzerland, as ideal for raising a large family.

Large in those days meant Geraldine, Michael, Josephine, Victoria and Eugene on the way.

Occasional cook, bottle washer, wardrobe mistress, nurse, travel escort, teacher and chauffeur to the present day septet, Miss Pyniger, known affectionately as Pinnie, was speaking for the first time of her life with Charlies Gang.

"You have to get used to thinking of them as an entity" she pointed out. They are exceptionally united and like all children of a large family, extremely good at raising each other.

As an example she quoted the gangs, deadly insult "Spoilt Brat". Loud protestations rent the air when this invective is banded around. At the moment it is sometimes addressed to Jane, that young lady, four in May, is slightly inclined to think that the world should give way to her whims. I'm not spoilt, she cries bitterly on such occasions. I'm not spoilt, I'm happy.

"And she won't be spoilt either" concludes Pinnie. The others see to it without interference and she'll grow up to loathe the very idea.

Junior education in this family includes the big ones teaching the little ones never to disturb father at work and to tiptoe past his study, discouraging cry babies and unanimously squashing any attempt to put on side because Daddy is famous.

It's miraculously effective. So much so that spoilt brats from the outside world are seldom invited to the white house with its immense park, swimming pool and shaded trees that is the childrens kingdom. Their parents accept their judgement.

Oona and Charlie allow the gang to pick any friends they like. At first Pinnie found it mildly disconcerting that the unwashed, tattered offspring of some unsavoury drunken labourer, near Corsier, the local village, should be as welcome or more so that many a child grown-ups would label "nice".

Then she noticed that instead of picking up bad habits the gang was pretty good – perhaps because of its own strength as a unit – at passing on what it considered norms of behaviour.

"Dis bonjour" say Good day. Tadpole (Eugene) aged seven will admonish some urchin, not polite enough to the Chaplin gardener, come on. Say it.

He is so determined that he always wins through. "The sort like his father" sums up Pinnie.

When he was younger the others used this resemblance to dress up Tadpole in a Woolworths "Charlie set"; flappy long sneakers, a cane, black moustache and that bowler, perched on Tadpoles outsize head, that no hat will fit, hence his nickname.

This love of theatricals inspired me to keep a special glory hole where every object suitable for dressing up is carefully hoarded.

Vicky, (Victoria } now 10, is the bravest of the lot. You can't frighten her. Her hobbies are dancing and playing the guitar quite remarkably well for her age. She with Tadpole and Josephine, age 12, set off by car every morning at half past seven for their school in Lausanne, 18 miles away and only return home in the late afternoon.

"It's a long day for such children, complained Pinnie; and seems even longer when we struggle through their homework together in the evenings. Me with my broad accent getting rather on Tadpoles nerves. He's fighting with French verbs and genders and tries to lift himself out of his chair by his hair when he gets all muddled up.

Josephine is the warmest hearted and has her mothers sunny smile. If you tell her to watch the baby you can be sure she won't move till you come back, whatever it costs her.

Curly haired toddler Jane and baby Annette, 16 months old, are the stay-at- homes who get the most maternal attention. The youngest of the family always sleeps downstairs, in the early months to have its last feed given by Oona, latter to enjoy breakfast with her and afternoon naps in her four poster bed-room. Each moves up to the top floor nursery quarters when the next one comes along. There is never any jealousy or resentment. The change over is so natural.

The two eldest again lead separate lives. Geraldine, nearly 17 and growing to be the living image of Oona, is still a tomboy. "Thank heaven" says Pinnie. She'll pose for photographers wearing her brother's gloves and be absolutely unconcerned about it. She is just going to her first dances and has an inordinate love for one black velvet dress. Don't wear it again. I beg her. People will think you have nothing else to put on.

This remark would break down the average teenager. Geraldine goes on wearing that dress and laughs. When we went to the mountains this last winter she did bring a party frock with her but forgot every accessory including an evening slip. Finally she managed to get ready for the expected dance looking simply lovely and wearing a brooch of mine in her hair as a makeshift trinket.

Geraldine dreams of being a ballet dancer but has bravely promised her parents to take her Matric first. This is near the last lap and everyone is watching her progress anxiously. A weekly boarder at a Lausanne school she is not a hard worker but before exams she always stays up late a weekends, brewing herself lots of coffee and working like mad. Then she sails through her tests.

She is also an experimenter—on others. She dabbed me all over my face with some miracle anti-headache cream that Russian guests had given her. It supposed to be used on the temples, the forehead and I think the chin, says Pinnie ruefully telling the story, but it worked.

Michael, 15, is the dreamer. He was so late to start reading that I spent hours with him wondering if we'd ever get anywhere. Now you can't pry him away from books, especially French poetry, she marvels and adds; he came back recently from his first week at a new Lausanne school with a most unpoetic vocabulary. Real Billingsgate.

"And what are you doing, young man?" I enquired.

He shrugged. "It's the unavoidable consequence of going to a boarding school" he pointed out rather smugly, not having wanted to go there in the first place.

224

It is the one educational handicap of the Chaplin young that they don't want to be separated and that, for that matter their parents don't want to let them go far away from home. First the local village school, now Lausanne, were chosen as half way alternatives, realising this Michael has settled down well to his studies.

Being a dreamer helped him to recover quickly from the excitement of film making. Acting in "A King in New York" might have gone to his head. After a fortnight he hardly remembered he'd been a star.

Pinnie however will not forget that film in a hurry. It involved unexpected occupational hazards for her. I was in charge of organising his screen wardrobe. That meant buying three of absolutely everything to be safeguarded against wear and tear and because he was going to be doused with water during one scene. The shop assistant thought we were mad. Then I had to take him to London for his medical check-up wanted for the Insurance purposes.

"Do you often have tonsillitis?" enquired the Doctor. With a wide grin Michael said, Yes. Which horribly complicated getting insurance coverage.

When the film started I wrote out all his dialogue on slips of paper and made him learn it by heart. That was bad enough, for both of us. But the worst moment was the hair-cut incident. Michael's hair was really getting too long and one Saturday I took him to the barbers near Great Fosters where the family was staying. Of course I gave instructions for only a light trim. He had to look more or less identical throughout the film. When the barber had finished I nearly burst into tears. He'd just about given him a crew cut.

Michael stared at himself in the mirror with equal dismay. " The continuity," he whispered. I thought, this is the end. I'll be fired the moment Mr Chaplin sets eyes on him. It can hold up production for weeks. We walked back to the hotel as slowly as possible. Mrs Chaplin took one look at Michael and said "for heavens sake, keep him out of his father's way".

For the rest of that day Michael stayed in hiding and crept up and down the back stairs. I finally retired to bed feeling that the end of the world- of this special, warm, wonderful Chaplin world had come to an end for me The next morning I told Michael. It's all useless. You can't hide from your father till your hair grows. Go and see him now. Michael went to his father's room and came out a little later. I was as nervously pacing the hall. " He never noticed". he said. Go in again and make him notice. I said. Mrs Chaplin later told me the end of the story. " Ha, you've had a hair cut, said Mr Chaplin, "That good. We are shooting the military school scenes next and I want your hair cropped".

This was positively the only time to date that my life with my beloved gang had been threatened.

I joined the family by one of those lucky chances that just happen to some people.

I was never trained either as a Nurse or a Governess, although I am now a mixture of both. In Canada I worked for the Winnipeg Hydro System. Later in England I also held secretarial posts, including several years in a job that brought me for the first time into closer contact with people, the Oxford University Womens Appointments Committee where I stayed till after World War II.

Liking people and children I then accepted a job to look after some English children in Switzerland, near Montreux. There I was rung up by the British Consulate. The Chaplin's were looking for a possible outings companion for their Scottish nanny KK [Edith McKenzie]. The two of us women arranged a meeting [we had already met outside the school]. Before she left for that first date Mrs Chaplin told KK, "if you like her, I'm treating you both to a dinner at any restaurant you choose".

"They've been as generous to both of us ever since" I said as an aside. We even have the use of a car on our days off. KK and I became firm friends. A little later when my job folded, I returned to England and was planning to sail for Canada on 17th November, 1953 when on the 13th a cable from the Chaplin's home asked her to help out for a few months. I felt I could not possible change my plans so late and walked with a friend to the nearest London Post Office to send a regretful refusal. They then turned homeward.

Suddenly I said, Do you think that the telegram has gone yet? We raced back. Too late. By now raring to go I seized a phone and asked for long distance. The day I was due to sail for Canada I caught a plane to Geneva instead. It was my very first flight.

Since then I have flown to Majorca, repeatedly to the South of France where the Chaplin's rent a villa at Cap Ferrat regularly for their holidays and to Paris to help Michael with his film dubbing, and often to England.

The last time the family flew into London Airport was when Charlie went for his 1960 fishing holiday in the Irish Republic.

The gang stepped off the plane to be met by a barrage of photographers and pressmen. They were the Important People, more so than their parents. They meant romance, charm, youth, the reality of that unbelievable lasting love between an elderly film genius and a woman 37 years his junior.

KK, a rather shy, auburn Aberdonian retired to the background clutching parcels and feeding bottles. I joined her, checking in my bag whether I had all the children's passports, which are always in my charge. Geraldine took the baby and put on her sunniest smile for the public. Josephine quirked an eyebrow at her eldest sister, Tadpole snorted.

Then just as the flashlights popped a steward came running across the tarmac waving two nappies the nurses had purposely left behind and never wanted to see again. They tried to push his offering back while he insisted "Yours, I think". Vicky began to giggle. An airport worker broke the tension, "Hey mate, keep them" he shouted, they may come in handy one day".

It was during this visit that I took all the older children to the East End of London. I knew it well from pre-war years I spent as secretary to the Superintendent of Spitalfields Market. I wanted them to see the heart of London, where their father had come from. They were deeply moved, their faces so serious and loving, as if they were more proud of him than ever. We also incidentally had a great welcome in every street we went.

The famous Savoy Hotel milk hunt also took place that holiday. Annette, the baby. was used to a Swiss formula and the nurses hadn't brought enough of her special brand. For one thing they hadn't planned on joining Charlie and Oona at their Irish fishing hotel. But they did; that family can't be kept apart for long.

Mrs Chaplin phoned, suggesting we join them. We had a nine hour drive from Belfast airport, I said. Dismay still in her voice, as well as laughter, she replied, "with all these young children, I don't know if you can imagine……..

But that is another story. Before returning to London I rang the Savoy to obtain two tins of the special Swiss milk food. Messenger boys scoured the town and finally able to deposit a package in my room. Only it wasn't there. The Page responsible was off duty and a great hunt through duchess's bedrooms took place; To everyone's great glee.

It was worth it to be back in London, I said afterwards. My affection for London is legendary among the junior Chaplin's.

At the Manior de Ban my light chintz covered room overlooking the lake contains one prize item of furniture. A screen. Here she tacks on all sorts of photographs and pictures, changing them as new events bring new interests to the children's lives. But there is always, in place of honour, a handkerchief with a design representing Piccadilly Circus.

"What's that?" asked Josephine once when she was younger. I began to explain about Picadilly being the centre of the world. Warming to my favourite subject I began to recite the long list of famous shops along Regent Street, my voice taking on the sort of rhythmic chant that goes with such a recital….. OH please, no Shakespeare, protested Josephine, reminded of poetry lessons.

Another time Vicky raised a laugh. I was showing a picture of Westminster Abbey. I know, she announced triumphantly, that's where you were born.

The children have one model held up to them. A Canadian childhood friend of mine was crippled by polio. They might hate her if she weren't chair ridden, as it is she is now part of family folklore. "How Helen could do that when she was six [or five or ten according to necessity] is the chant chorused by the gang when one of their number thinks he or she had accomplished something exceptional.

Another more mundane clamour is for my Brownie chocolate cake, the family favourite. It's baking is a regular Tuesday event. On this, the cook's day off, I take over in the mornings to make the Canadian and American cookies and goodies that no continental chef would know about. In the evenings Oona, a wonderful cook, smilingly prepares dinner.

This is a family where the meaning of a light snack is unknown, agrees Kay Kay and me. These children gobble up everything in sight.

Healthy young appetites mean that Tuesday is the favourite day of the week. So much so that by unanimous decision its magic was recaptured for longer at the mountain chalet the Chaplin's rented this last winter at Crans.

There the outside help was a daily cleaning woman and these unbelievably unspoilt children of a millionaire rejoiced in helping with the chores, while the nurses coped without a murmur.

But then there are two incredibly attractive reasons why any woman in her right mind would enjoy working for the Chaplin's. They are........ The Gang and their parents who brought them up this way.

Chapter Thirteen

It was late September 1973, one late afternoon when it had been a very hot day. I was in my room resting with my feet up. There was a tap at the door. I called "come in" and Mrs Chaplin entered asking if she could have a few words. This was the first time I had seen her since her return from Paris. She came over to the window and sat down beside me.

She inquired if I was well and said that she was glad that they were home as Paris was so busy and the traffic horrific. She went on to inquire if I had received her letter, as this was what she wished to talk to me about. She looked very uncomfortable and no doubt she did not relish the task.

You know Pinnie, it took me several weeks to make up my mind to do it, but as you know things could not go on as they were. Please forgive me for doing it that way, I could not face you, or KK for that matter. Our family is now going their own ways and there is not enough work for two of you. You know the situation as well as I do, we have been together for over 20 years, we have had our ups and downs, although not seriously affecting our relationship. Both my husband and I appreciate your dedication to the children and to the whole family including our relations and friends. We have become friends ourselves and because of that I wish that your leaving should not be as an ordinary employee to an employer. We still wish to see you often and the door will always be open to you.

We were talking about you last night at supper with Nicky and Josie. As you perhaps already know their marriage is going through a difficult period and they have agreed to live apart for some time. Josie will be going to Paris and Nicky will be living in his flat in Geneva with young Charlie. He would like you to take over the responsibility of Governess and Companion to his son Charlie for a period that it is impossible to say. There is a service flat next to Nicky's that is empty, which would be yours if you take on the job. Of course, you could spend some time with us here if you preferred, with Charlie who would be a great companion to Christopher.

I listened to her talking; I didn't say a word. Here again was an offer quite out of the blue. What was I to do? Did I feel capable of taking on a very lively child at my age? The job offered me a flat of my own. All these things raced through my mind as I sat there thinking about furniture, salary etc? I had been to Nicky's flat several times with young Charlie and always thought what a nice modern flat it was, situated just outside Geneva City in the commune of Grand Saconnex, quite near the Airport. Number 20 Chemin du Pommier was about three floors up, overlooking a park; it had its own private swimming pool. When I said that I did not have any furniture of my own and that I would have to shop around for some second-hand pieces, Mrs Chaplin said I could take what I needed from the top floor of the Manoir, as for salary I should talk to Nicky about that.

I took the plunge and said that I would take the position if Nicky were happy about it. Glory be! Someone was again looking after me. Mrs Chaplin left me to think about it all. I was over the moon. My lifestyle would be much the same and I would be with my friends in Geneva.

The next time I saw Nicky he offered me a very reasonable salary and confirmed all that had been said, saying I could move in at my own time at the same time looking after Charlie, either at the Manoir or in Geneva.

The news got around and the children were told of my eventual departure. All of them, without exception, were dumbstruck to think that I would be leaving the family. I was family and had been for a long time. The younger ones implored me to stay. Christopher and Annette were reduced to tears but cheered up when I explained that I would still be seeing them quite often when I came to the Manoir with young Charlie.

During the next few weeks I started packing my personal belongings; collected over the past 20 years. To most people it was junk but to me it was my personal recollections of very happy times. As for furniture Mrs Chaplin agreed for me to take several small side tables, dinning chairs, including a very large comfortable armchair that she said she would be glad to get rid of, as it was the property of Paulette Goddard, her husband's ex-wife. Her name was written on the frame underneath. Each time someone visited me I offered them Paulette Goddard's chair, it was a great joke. Mrs Chaplin also gave me cupboards, curtains and mats. The only things I should have to buy were bed linen etc.

During this time I met Max Reinhart and his wife together with Claire Bloom with husband Elride and daughter Ann, who were visiting the Chaplin's.

Mrs Chaplin offered me the use of the large car together with driver Renato to take my things to the new flat. He commented that I looked like the "A Jew from Russia" with my many parcels tied up with string. Off we went and very soon had unloaded all my things. Let's have a cup of tea! Yes please, said Renato. Oh dear, no tea, milk or sugar; this was my first experience of having to plan in advance for myself the everyday necessities of keeping house.

The following weeks in the run up to Xmas I was busy organising my apartment and seeing to Charlie who was now at his new school. We could walk there each day as it was nearly opposite our flat. I had the pleasure of meeting John Sistovaris, an uncle of Nicky who had a furrier shop in Winnipeg. The carol service at Charlies new school was wonderful and we all made arrangements to spend Christmas together in Nicky's flat. Nicky gave me a new TV set that I enjoyed immensely.

1974 was to be a year where I was *toing and froing* between Geneva and Vevey, doing my usual work with Charlie. Some weekends Nicky would take Charlie out to various places which gave me free time. Morvydd, one of my best friends, took me to visit the "World Council of Churches" where she worked. There I met many of her other friends who invited me to join the Protestant Churches Womens Guild. They met each month to foster the understanding of women worldwide. It was with them that I began to study the Bible in depth and to try to understand the religious practices of other people in the world.

Late February I flew to Brussels to visit the Marbach family and to see dear, first child Nenette, who by now was a qualified nurse working in London. I took the opportunity to visit the Ensore Exhibition and to take communion at the Holy Trinity Church.

Back home for pancake day. Charlie loved them. Also news that Tad would marry in August.

KK rang to say everyone was invited to Ireland for the usual fishing and holiday break for Mr and Mrs Chaplin. Ireland was the only place where they could get around without the interference of the Press. Of course we were delighted to go and arrived in southern Ireland on April 1st. Fresh air, good company, good food and quietness. Donkey rides, fishing and pony riding over the moors. We stayed until19th April. A very welcome break.

Back home to Geneva to stay a few days in the Manoir. Here I met the Ex Queen Maria Jose` of Italy with her son the Prince Victor Emmanuel age 2 years.

July was my holiday time and when KK said she could look after Charlie I was able to fly to Inverness, Scotland staying with Mrs Cowie at Kinloss. Flying north always brought on a bout of rheumatism. Mrs Cowie lined my bed with hot water bottles saying that this would do the trick. She took me to visit Lock Ness and fort Augustus, also the home of the Duke of Richmond and Gordon and Lady Cork from Eton. The site of the battle of Culloden with the Clava stones made a very interesting day out. I returned to Edinburgh and flew south to London where I saw the Lord Mayors show, met Joy Holmes, daughter of Hartley and then on to Hampshire to visit my relations. The usual round of hellos and goodbyes, endless cups of good tea and I was off home to Geneva.

On 9th August we all went up to Corsier to witness the civil wedding of Eugene and Sandra. Afterwards we all had lunch at St Saphorin. This restaurant you will have guessed was a great favourite of ours.

Nicky had taken delivery of a new Jaguar car and was caught speeding at 130kph in a restricted zone. Oh dear!

Christmas this year was to be at the Manoir. All the Chaplin's, and Sistovaris family were invited. Most of them turned up together with the new additions. As usual it was delightful and I enjoyed being with them all again.

On 28th we all departed for Crans Montana for the Winter Sports. Staying in Elfie's Chalet.

1975. New Year in Crans Montana was a special treat as the town put on a snow carnival, bright lights at night and many fireworks. Everybody dresses up and parties go on everywhere. I slipped up and hurt my arm falling on the floor. Dr Barros was called and he gave me pills after putting a bandage on my arm.

We all returned to the Manoir to get back to normal when Mr and Mrs Chaplin were visited by a representative of the United Kingdom Government who said that the Queen would like to honour him in recognition of his great work in the British film and music world. Of course Mr Chaplin was dumbfounded; yes, he had been born a British citizen but had spent a number of his early years in America. He considered this the greatest honour in his life. Most of the family, unfortunately not me, set off for the Savoy in London. March 4th was the great day when the family went to Buckingham Palace. Mr Chaplin was ushered in and escorted to the waiting room, there together with many other people who were to be honoured they were instructed on the etiquette and formalities to be used during the ceremony. Mr Chaplin was called before the Queen who invested him with a Knighthood, he would now be addressed as Sir Charles Chaplin and Mrs Chaplin would be Lady Chaplin. Afterwards the family had their photograph taken outside the Palace and outside the Savoy Hotel.

Back home we all set off for a few days to visit Venice by train. With me taking charge of Charlie we arrived at 9.35 pm. both tired and hungry. After a good meal we retired to bed and were up next morning ready to see the city by boat taxi.

Glass making was very interesting and we bought a present for Nicky. St Marks square was beautiful. We stayed for five days and then set off for Milan by a new train with all glass interconnecting doors. One of these flew back and hit me in the face, very nasty, the train company got first-aid and offered to pay for me to see a doctor on my arrival in Milan.

Back home in Geneva, Charlie returned to school that gave me plenty of spare time. Each day I visited friends or friends came to me. Morvydd came many times and we usually went out to various places of interest, taking in lunch at restaurants all over town. YaYa, Mr Sistovaris [senior] sister, came with us sometimes; she was a very interesting lady and I enjoyed her company. All three of us went to the World Council of Churches for a meeting of the International Christian Womens Club where I met the President of the Swiss Confederation, Mr Pierre Grarer.

In June we set off for Greece with Nicky. Staying at Galexidi. Nia and Katia Sistovaris Elfie and YaYa made up the party. Young Charlie enjoyed the swimming in the beautiful, blue clear water. Went to Delphi and took the waters there. Bought a book on Greek mythology.

August came with a visit by Josie from Paris. There was no doubt that divorce proceedings were in the offing, black faces everywhere. Nicky very upset and kept to himself quite a lot. Josie took off for Yugoslavia in a huff. Apparently the Greek laws on divorce do not favour the wife. The children always stay with the father.

August was, of course, my personal holiday time. Charlie was in Greece with his father. Off I went to England and stayed with my cousin Rose at Meonstoke, in the Meon river valley. Here was peace and tranquillity and I settled down to letter writing to Canada, preparing the way for my planned visit next year. Tea with the locals and communion on Sunday at the local St Andrews Church. Spent one day with Ken and Audrey at Bishops Waltham. Other days we visited Lee-on-Solent and the Isle of Wight where we stayed at the Winterbourne Hotel, Bonchurch. Lunch of fresh crab a speciality.

During the many times I returned to the U.K. I always stayed with cousin Rose but later when she got older I stayed with Audrey and Ken at Bishops Waltham. Audrey always managed to get some time off from work and we would take the car to visit either friends or beautiful places. Oxford to visit the Twinnings, also to Poole in Dorset to visit my old friend Dorothy then on to Bournemouth to stay at the St Georges Hotel again. Audrey took me around Dorset to visit the National Trust property at Kingston Lacy, the New Forest and Milford-on-Sea. Another year, Audrey took me all the way down to the west of England, to stay at her sisters hotel, Bovey House Hotel, near Beer, then continuing on to the village of Polzeath in north Cornwall where we stayed for 5 days.

I returned to Geneva to supervise Charlie on his return to school on September 12th. Here I ran into a spot of trouble. Charlie refused to go. He ran around the flat refusing to be persuaded to change his mind. He was not going to school and that was that. He hated it and all the teachers. It was not until the 23rd that he could be coaxed to return, something was very much amiss. The divorce, no Mother, perhaps that was the problem? Was I doing my job correctly? He really needed a younger person. On 2nd October I saw Lady Chaplin and discussed with her the problem with Charlie. She went out and bought him a new bicycle, perhaps that would cheer him up? Eugene and Sandra were at the Manor, which was good for Charlie as he felt more at home with younger people.

November was the second anniversary of my joining the Sistovaris family. Nicky gave me 10 red roses. And we all had lunch at Chambery to celebrate.

Christmas was at the Manoir. With all present except Josie. Sir Charles was very feeble. Afterward we all sat down to watch "Limelight". So ended 1975.

Nicky was away in Leningrad, buying furs and was not home until the end of January. During February Nicky told me that he would be giving up the flat but he had negotiated another in the older part of Geneva, at Florissant; he assured me the Flat was large enough for all three of us to live there. The move was due to the forthcoming divorce. This was difficult for me as I had to put all my furniture that I had accumulated in storage until I retired properly. However, we all moved as planned but Nicky during this time was going through a period of depression due no doubt to the terms of the divorce. Sometimes he would come home worse for drink. This made it very difficult for me to explain to Charlie what was going on.

During June my eyes began to play up. My Doctor said that my blood pressure was too high and gave me pills to rectify it. My visit to the hospital revealed that I had cataracts but that I should come back in two months to see if they were getting worse. I bought some darker glasses which helped, but the Doctor said that I should take life a little slower and calmer. What a hope!

During July we all took off for Greece, staying at Patras. Nicky was seeing his lawyers every day, but mother Sistovaris was kindness itself. We visited all the usual places and Charlie enjoyed the swimming etc.

November was the time when I had planned to return to Canada, perhaps for the last time. Just a short visit of course; but I felt I must go before my health prevented it. On the 16th I had packed everything I thought I would need and was ready to go. The next day I had lunch with a few of my friends and many more phoned me wishing me a safe journey.

CHAPTER FOURTEEN

The large Boeing aircraft took off from London Heathrow at about 6.30 p.m. I settled into my seat happy that I was returning to my true home. All my friends had been informed by letter of my arrival and would, no doubt be making arrangements for me to return to my old haunts. Lady Chaplin had very kindly given me 750sf to help with expenses, she was always very kind! After flying all night we landed at Montreal on 19th November to a howling snowstorm, nevertheless there was a welcoming party waiting at arrival.

Five friends were waiting and after tearful re-unions we took a taxi to the home of Emily Hay, an old friend from League of Tramps days. Here I was to stay for as long as I liked. That night, however we all brought ourselves up to date with all our lives; some friends had married of course and had homes in Montreal, Toronto and Ottawa with many others in British Columbia. I would catch up with these in due course. I started on a grand tour of the surrounding area, weather permitting. It was gratifying to realise that my friends still held my friendship the same as ever. Never was I happier than with them in Canada.

On 3rd December I moved on to Winnipeg. Here again I was welcomed by some of my old school friends. My main job here was to see that my fathers grave was being properly looked after, which it was, the grass was all cut and the stone had been cleaned. I went into the quietness of St Johns Cathedral and knelt down to say a few prayers. Oh, how I wished things had been different in my early days. I had seen so many happy families, why was I subjected to family discord? However, God had been good to me and for that I was thankful. I walked up the aisle and looked at the stained glass windows I had been so familiar with in my youth. For some reason I did not wish to stay long in Winnipeg and the following day took a flight to Vancouver. I booked into the North Plaza Hotel and contacted my very good friend Helen who was still running the dress shop. We arranged a number of outings visiting Stanley Park, the Theatre and Art Galleries. Lunch, of course was always at the "White Spot" and usually with oysters.

She introduced me to her friends Sybil and Bill Wilson, who lived nearby. They invited us all to their house for Christmas, it was the usual English fare with Xmas pudding and minced pies, yummy.

My time in Canada was running out. I had seen for the last time my old haunts and most of my old friends but something told me that I had been away so long that the new Canada was not for me. I looked forward to returning to Europe. 1st January 1977 saw me on a return flight direct to Geneva.

Back in the new flat, everything was array, the whole place wanted tidying up and cleaning. So I set about this straight away. Charlie was pleased to see me and gave me kisses. In the post was a letter from Josie, cancelling her arrangement with me to look after Charlie. What a shock! Nicky said to ignore the letter, but it did upset me.

In due course I was able to go to visit my local friends and went to Les Avants to see Ann Hodgeson and Jean Vicario who was now living in the top flat above. Down in Corsier at the Manoir; auntie Gypsy was the guest and she, KK and myself with Charlie went out to lunch at St Saphron, always a great treat. Auntie Gypsy told us that the Eugene and Sandra marriage was going through a bad patch. They had agreed to three months separation.

25th January, was Charlies 6th birthday, we held a party with local children and what a great success it was. Nicky was upset because he could not go to Leningrad as usual because, I think, of his divorce terms or perhaps of the political situation in Russia.

I was at the Manoir with Charlie when an official letter came for me from the Swiss Government saying that my work and residence permit had expired, when would I be leaving the country? If I wished to remain I was to apply for a renewal within 14 days.

Eugene and Sandra were for once together at the Manoir and they helped me to fill in the forms for the renewal which were sent off together with the fee. A renewal was duly issued to last up to March 1985.

The months seemed to slip by and I welcomed a short holiday in Malta and Gozo with Nicky and Charlie. We stayed at a British hotel overlooking the harbour; lots of warships were in the harbour including the Aircraft carrier Hermes, together with Frigates and Destroyers.

During June Nicky said I was to take Charlie up to the Manoir, where everyone was preparing for the great "Fete de Vigneron", in the town of Vevey. All the local school children were required to take part together with all the towns various organisations. The Swiss are a fortunate people, low taxes, stunning views, and access to locally produced white, red and rose wines, surprising in their quality and variety. This wine culture is cause for celebration at an event that occurs just four times in each century and is of national and international importance. The Fete dates back to 1783. The festival is organised by the Brotherhood of Winegrowers of Vevey in the Canton of Vaud. To promote the cultivation of, and improve the methods of the wine growers and to honour its finest artisans. The Brotherhood entrusts the festival to professional artists and they bring to the Fete good Music, Colour, Singing and general bonhomie to the visitors.

Sir Charles was asked to compose some music for the festival, which he did. He spent many weeks in his study and then presented it to the festival as his contribution to the event and his appreciation of living in their delightful countryside.

My job was to see that the children got to their allocated places at the correct time and to help with the dance routines. Three national orchestras, 5000 actors [not all professional] had Radio and TV coverage. The arena in the central car park and market place was transformed into a giant theatre with a backdrop to the lake. It was indeed a beautiful setting. The actual Fete took place during late July for a whole week, when everyone for miles around came to Vevey for the event including many overseas visitors.

During September we all went to Cannes for a short holiday visiting the Picasso museum, St Paul de Vence and Grasse, where we all bought perfume.

Remembrance Day was celebrated at my local church and it was there I met what was to become my very dear friend Bobbie. Bobbie was the widow of a Royal Air Force officer who was also a stockbroker; after his death in London she came to Geneva to live with her daughter. She and I attended church regularly and it was through her that I was invited to my first prayer meeting. These meetings were to become part of my life from here on. I received great comfort from them and met many new friends.

November came in very cold and one day Nicky came home with a fur coat that was surplus and said if it fitted me I could have it. What joy! It fitted me perfectly .I wore it every winter from there on.

The Court ruling on Nicky's divorce gave judgement that prevented Josie from taking Charlie into France. I imagined that I would not see much of Josie from now on. What a shame, I loved her dearly.

My friend Morveth was very ill about this time and I paid regular visits to her home to try to comfort her. But the biggest shock of all came by telephone from the Manoir on Christmas day. KK reported that Sir Charles had died. I immediately went to my church to offer prayers for him and Lady Chaplin. The next day being Monday I went up to the Manoir to see Lady Chaplin and went on to see Ann Hodgeson at Les Avants where I stayed in order to be close to the Manoir for the funeral. On the day of the funeral I was invited to follow the family with KK in one of the funeral cars. The service was very moving and the flowers were magnificent, covering great areas of the churchyard. The English film personalities were very much in the majority together with many political personalities.

This was indeed the end of an era that had dominated 25 years of my life. Would my relations with the Chaplin's continue? I had moved out of their house and was now living with another family. I need not have worried, for Lady Chaplin wrote to me in reply to my condolence letter saying that she wished everything to go on as before and to look upon the Manoir as my second home.

Nicky, Charlie and I spent the new year at Gstaad. Charlie skiing most of the time. The snow was perfect but I refrained from the sport as I felt it was time to give it up. I was now 72 and was finding looking after children very tiring and worrying. I resolved to speak to Nicky about this.

I had been invited to England to the wedding of Ken and Audrey's youngest son Stuart, who was to marry a local girl Penny Shepherd. I therefore set of for England staying with my cousin Rose as usual. The service was held at St Peters Church, Bishops Waltham and afterwards a reception at the local golf club. I took the opportunity, of course, to visit my relatives and friends. I particularly enjoyed walking at Lee-on-Solent seafront where the air was keen and salty but I made sure I did not miss my lunch and drinks at the Osborne View Hotel.

On my return to Geneva I set about cleaning the flat and catching up on my mail and other jobs. I could not have been more surprised and disgusted when KK rang to say that robbers had dug up and stolen the coffin of Sir Charles and were demanding a ransom for its return. Oh God! What is the world coming to?

Early March was the week of Womens World Day of Prayer. We all went to the Cathedral where I said some special prayers for Lady Chaplin, who must be feeling awful. Later we had supper with Johannes, Elsie and Kaki, some friends of Bobbies where I was introduced as "Little Charlies Nanny". Glory be. How rude can people get.

As I said, I would have a word with Nicky about my future. One evening he took me out to Ferney in France for dinner. I thought it was a good time to broach the subject. He told me that since his divorce was about to become absolute, he had been planning a great change in his life. Charlie was growing up and it was a good time to send him to a boarding school, where there would be greater prospects than at his local school. Also, because of the divorce the lease on the flat would expire.

244

He advised me to look for another flat to call my own, and that I ought to consider complete retirement. He was right, of course. Carmel, who worked at the "United Nations" as a secretary, came to my rescue. She had secured a flat from the local commune at Grand Sacconex and advised me to put my name down for the next vacancy. In the meantime I stayed at Nicky's flat and after Charlie went to boarding school, my time was for the first time all completely my own.

I decided to go the England and this time by train. I took the express to Paris and onto Boulogne where I caught the overnight ferry to Dover. I then went on to Eastbourne where I stayed at the same hotel as before. Two days here and then off to Roses bungalow in Hampshire. She suggested a great idea, what about a trip to the Isle of Man? Fantastic, when? Now, said Rose, and we will invite my sister-in-law Kathy Houghton to come with us. July 31st saw us in Douglas, the main town. Roses old friends the Begbees, who were in business there, took us around the Island. We all had a great time as the weather was sunny all the time.

When I got back to Geneva I had a pleasant surprise. In the post was a cheque for 1117.80sf being my half yearly annuity from Canada.

Ken and Audrey, from England, had arrived in Switzerland on their annual holiday and were staying at the Hotel Famille in Vevey. This was the home of my friend Madame Krachenbuhl where we took tea on many occasions. I arranged to show them all the better sights of the locality. Ken even came up to the Manoir with me to swim in the pool.

A letter arrived from Paris from Josie saying that I should vacate the flat as soon as possible, according to the divorce settlement. This annoyed Nicky terribly. But as I have said before, someone was guiding me and by the very next post a letter arrived from the Commune to say that a flat was available and if I came to their office the tenancy could be discussed. I went as soon as possible and inspected the property. It was a large single room with adjoining bathroom and kitchen; it could be described as a bedsit. It was on the seventh floor with a lift to all levels complete with security entrance. The view to the south was fantastic, across a park and the city, across to the lake and on a clear day they said you could see Mont Blanc. I signed the documents at once and agreed to move in as soon as possible. The address was No 21. Chemin de Taverney.

At last I had my own home after 73 years. I got my furniture out of store and proceeded to make a home for myself. Gifts from a lot of friends contributed to the effect. I held a small party to celebrate, mostly friends from my church and prayer meetings. Do not think it was a dull get together, they were all full of fun with not a bible in sight.

Most of 1979 was taken up with socialising with friends in Geneva and the Vevey district. I have mentioned quite a lot of names who the reader will not recognise and are not part of my regular life but being a person who likes to talk to people and to listen to their stories I was always out and about at many places, lunches, dinners and suppers, the list is immense. I was pleased to have friends from the third world countries, they brought a new perspective to my outlook on life. I kept a visitors book that I asked everyone to write in when they came to see me. Looking back it makes good reading and refreshes my memory.

There were several highlights of the year that I should mention. A trip to Derbyshire in England and the surrounding countryside. Worchester and Oxford to see my mother's grave. Penhurst Place and Westerham in Kent. London for the Trooping of the Colours in Horse Guards Parade with the Queen in attendance, a very colourful affair.

While in London I went to see Vicky in her new venture, the "Circus Imaginaire" at the Riverside Studios. It was very good and we had drinks afterwards with her husband Jean

Baptiste. I shall always remember the time that Audrey and Ken were visiting me at the Manoir, Vicky was arranging the music for the show at the time and when they arrived a bee had stung Christopher and the house was in turmoil.

A week in Lugano, with visits to a beautiful village called Morcote and then Lake Como. The Italian atmosphere of this area is ideal for me as I love the warm weather.

A few days later I spent the whole day watching the funeral of Lord Louis Mountbatten on TV (he had been murdered in southern Ireland). That night I sat down to write condolence letters to his family at Broadlands Estate, Romsey, quite near Roses home. Also to the Queen who was his niece.

Back in Geneva I was invited to bring Charlie to a party at the home of Prince Victor Emmanuelle. It was his son's birthday. After the party I rang Nicky to pick us up but there was no reply. Instead, the Prince drove us home himself in his Mercedes. Wow!. What fun to be driven by Royalty.

On 22nd December I flew to England to spend Christmas with Rose. Listened to the Queens speech after lunch and went to her daughters' home for tea. So ended the year and I went home to Taverney. Morveth was waiting for me at the airport. We spent the evening together very quietly.

The new year 1980 started very quietly for me. I was visiting friends and then entertaining them at my home. I was most surprised, however, when an important envelope arrived by post. It was from the Chairman and Council of the British Residents Association inviting me to a reception at the Palais de Beaulieu, Lausanne on the occasion of the State Visit to Switzerland of Her Majesty The Queen and His Royal Highness The Duke of Edinburgh. To be held on Wednesday 30th April 1980, from 3.15 pm. to 4.15 pm. Glory be! Of course I would be there, come hell or high water.

The great day came and I donned my best outfit and bought a new hat. Treated myself to a taxi to Lausanne and presented myself at the entrance. I took along my grandfather's swagger stick with an engraved silver top that he had had in the army. It helped me along as a walking stick. Past the Swiss police, past the British soldiers in their dress outfits, I was very proud to be British that day. I took tea and fancy cakes and awaited the arrival of Her Majesty. Many people were there and I was afraid I would not see her. But I need not have worried, they made their way in my direction, talking to people as they went, before long they were opposite me and I got myself in the front. They came over directly towards me and Her Majesty asked me my name and where I lived in Switzerland; we shook hands and she passed on. The Duke however took much longer and came up to me with a laugh; where did you get that stick? he said. It was my grandfathers, I said, when he was a Sergeant Major at Camberley in 1905. He looked at the silver top and said it was beautiful and then gave it a twirl and handed it back to me. I was "over the moon", what a story to tell my friends.

After another few months I decided to go to England again. This time direct to Bournemouth, staying as usual at St Georges Hotel. They knew me now as an old customer and looked after me well. I stayed a week and then went up to Oxford to stay with my friend Betty Twinning and her two sisters. Checked out Mothers grave and after a week returned to London. Tea at Fortnum and Masons and took in a few shows.

Lady Chaplin phoned to say they would be unveiling a statue of Sir Charles in Corsier and would she like to come along? There I met Mr and Mrs Sydney Chaplin and Betty Tetrick and four of the children. We all went back afterwards for tea at the Manoir.

During December I was taken by Martin and Shirley Buchmann, more friends, to a carol service at the Chapel in the W.C.C. in Geneva. It was beautiful, with three choirs and two orchestras.

Christmas was spent at my friend Ann Cantors house. She was with her family, Daniel, David, Joshua, Alan and Norrie. Lunch at 3 pm.

1981 came in with marvellous sunsets, showing the top snow on Mt Blanc in full relief, several evenings in a row. I went up to Vevey to my bank to check things out and calculated that my income was satisfactory to continue living as I was. Went on up to Les Avants to stay with Ann Hodgeson. Met Emile Babler, a gifted singer and pianist who fled from Austria during the war.

Hot news the next day. Prince Charles got engaged to Lady Diana Spencer. This called for a letter of congratulations to Buckingham Palace.

Cousin Rose meanwhile, in England, had been admitted to a nursing home as she was getting frailer every month. I thought that I must go to see her and on April 1st flew to London where I stayed for a few days at the Commonwealth Club, then back to Ken and Audreys. My visit to the nursing home convinced me that Rose was getting weaker by the day, she was my foremost relation in England, and it was she who first met me on my arrival in England. We were about the same age and got on well together. It pained me to see her so frail. One day while I was visiting some other relations I got news that she had passed away. I had purchased my return tickets to Switzerland that was due in two days time. Audrey said that there was nothing that I could do by staying on and I should go as planned. I arranged for a lovely wreath to be placed by her grave and reluctantly left England. My dear cousin was gone and I would miss her very much.

Back home the commune issued free geraniums for the decoration of all our window boxes that created a wonderful display all summer. The block of flats looked beautiful. It was with some shock that I read in the evening paper that Mr Sistovaris had been shot while leaving a casino at Evian in France. He always went there to gamble as there was no restriction on the amount of money you could use. He was taken to hospital but died later on. Nicky was devastated, so was young Charlie. The funeral coming so soon after Roses upset me terribly.

I settled down to a more quite life in my flat but I continued to entertained several people each week. I could not live without company. I looked forward to my prayer meetings in other friends flats where I continued to meet many new people from all over the world.

January 1982 brought news from the Department of Pensions to advise me of an increase in my Swiss pension of 51sf. A few days later a similar letter from the British Department of Pensions to say that my pension had been increased to £32.85 per week. I thought it was time to review my will and went to my solicitor to do this. I also thought I should go to England to settle my English account at the bank. I therefore went to the U.K during April staying, of course, at Audreys. I wished to go to Fareham where my mother lived before she married. Trinity Street was still there but No 32 had been pulled down and built over with a Police Station. Ironical I thought. I went in to Trinity Church to sit down to remember my mother.

For many weeks now I had been thinking of going back to Canada. I know that I had decided that the last visit would be my last but I had an urge to go again. If I did not go now it would be too late. I therefore booked a return flight with BA leaving on September 17th to Calgary.

CHAPTER FIFTEEN

I arrived in Calgary in bright sunshine. The view over a lake to the mountains was terrific. The Palliser hotel looked out over the Bow River and was extremely comfortable. My first outing on the Sunday was to St James Church where I took communion. An old friend from school days met me and in her car showed me all over the city ending with a meal in a Chinese Restaurant. After three days I went with a coach party to Sulpher mountain by a gondola and then joined the main highway north to a Buffalo reserve to the Banff Springs Hotel, then on to Lake Louise and the Columbian Icefields - saw wild goats, beaver lodges and wild geese and also Jasper and Whistler Mountain; supper at the Jasper Park Lodge.

Returning to Calgary I flew to Vancouver to be met by Louise and Tom Thompson who took me to my hotel. The following day we went on a trip up the Frazer and Thompson rivers staying at an old Ranch House that was freezing cold. We eventually found the spot where the salmon come to spawn and die; a four year cycle. Bears feed on the dead fish so that we were escorted for safety by a Park Ranger. This is a very beautiful uninhabited area; the mountains, rivers and wildlife were a real tonic to me, so different from Switzerland where even the high mountains are inhabited.

I returned to Vancouver for another two days, where I booked myself on a Greyhound Coach tour of northern U.S.A. leaving Seattle in two days time.

Pinnies records in her diaries of this trip are very few and far between, but by her photographs she visited most of the northern states finishing in New York where she flew back to Geneva. Her friends said she should not have done this trip, she was mad, she would kill herself or have a heart attack. But there, as she said, she was an itinerate traveller.

This must have been a major effort for a person of 76 years of age. What writings she made in her diaries had become almost impossible to read, her eyesight was deteriorating which did not help. But she was a very determined person who when she made up her mind to do something she always did it. This was her last contact with Canada and from then on said that it was not like it used to be, not like her memories of her youth but as they say, Time marches on. And we must accept change, be it for better or worse.

It was nice to be home with my regular friends, my little flat was cosy and warm and I was very happy there. During late December my friend Madame Krahenbuhl of the Famille Hotel in Vevey invited me there for the New Year. This was very kind of her as the hotel was always busy at that time of the year. But everything was found for me and I enjoyed it immensely.

On January 1st 1983 Michael phoned to wish me a happy new year. I was so pleased that my eldest boy never forgot me. He phoned on every anniversary; he was so kind.

During the next six months my life revolved around my local friends and I "slowed down" as the doctor had asked. But every week there was something going on, first there was my bible studies then my monthly outings with the Skylarks, trips on the lake, excursions into the mountains, theatre trips and cinema. My closest friends invited me to their homes for meals. My close friend Bobbie had taken a new flat near the station and it was fun to go there to see her settled in.

During August I began to get an urge to go to England to see my family. I thought I felt fit enough and arranged to fly to London where I was met by a taxi who took me to Hampshire, staying with Ken and Audrey. I visited all my relations who took me to various places of interest and then to some very good places to eat. I remember having dinner one fine evening on the veranda of a yacht club looking out over the Solent to the Isle-of-Wight; it was magical in the fading light. I stayed about a week and then moved on to London where I went, of course, to Fortnum & Mason for tea. Then on to Harvey Nichols store to meet Nennette.

Back home I had a tea party for Mary, Carmel, Morveth and Bobbie, who were my nearest friends. Life continued as usual with no major trips or events. I was pleased however to learn that Audrey and Ken would be coming to me for Christmas. This would be the first time I had had any of my family for Christmas. They brought everything with them, food and wine complete, 7lbs of best English beef, vegetables and home made Christmas pudding.

A letter arrived early in 1984 from Madame Waks in Belgium asking if I would accompany her on a holiday to Minorca. She did not want to go alone as she had lost her husband the previous year. I would be a companion for her, would I please say yes. I telephoned her and discussed the holiday, dates etc. I agreed to go and a few days later flew with her to Majorca and then on to Minorca. We had a delightful holiday, the weather was good with roses being in bloom everywhere, If I remember rightly the hotel was called "Le Messidor", we visited Puerto Banyus, Marbella, a Fair in a bull ring and the mountains with glorious views over the Island. One day we took a boat journey along the coast to the mainland at Algeciras with a good view of Gibraltar, stayed one night and back to Minorca the next.

Back in Geneva I found my eyes were giving me trouble. A visit to the eye specialist who diagnosed cataracts which would have to be removed as soon as possible. In the meantime I was to use drops in my eyes each day. Oh Dear! What with my legs, high blood pressure and now eyes, it bought me down to earth with a bump. I must take things easier.

Easier did I say? Well, one day I again received a letter from the Lord Chamberlains Office in London, inviting me to Royal Garden Party to be held at Buckingham Palace on 17th July, 4- 6 p.m. The Queen Mother and the Prince of Wales will be present on the Queens behalf. Would I go? You bet I would. I would not miss an opportunity of seeing the dear Queen Mother who had remained in London with me and all of us during the terrible air raids during the war. I might even see Prince Charles. I had of course, sent a letter to the Queen, congratulating her on her 58 birthday.

On 13th I flew to London and booked into the Commonwealth Club as usual. Donning my best outfit I set of for the Palace. It was a lovely day and everyone was in morning dress, they all looked very smart. I mingled and chatted, moved where I thought the Royal party would go and awaited events. Sure enough the Prince appeared with the Queen Mother on his arm. They moved everywhere where I was not. But I did see them both at fairly close quarters at one period. I found myself talking to a gentleman at one point, who introduced himself by his first name. Whilst we talked another gentleman came up to us and began to make conversation. He referred to the other gentleman as the Bishop. Bishop! I said. Oh, I am so sorry, I did not know. He was the Bishop of York. I told him about my relationship with Bishop Matheson of Winnipeg and how he helped me during my education. We had a long talk and suggested we meet again to continue my story.

Whilst I was in the U.K. I went up to Oxford to see my friends the Twinnings and to check on Mothers grave. Then back to Ken and Audreys for a few days. Flying back to Geneva during August.

I realised I should take things easier and for the next few months did just that. I attended my prayer meetings as usual and occasionally entertained people from other countries who were lonely in Geneva, a cup of tea and a chat worked wonders. They all wrote in my visitors book a little tribute to remember them by.

January 29th 1980. 9.35 p.m.

Pinnie- hic!! Thanks for another lovely evening- you have had a busy day- film producers and chauffeurs, with KK, typically you. Love as always. Carmel.

November 19th 1980.

Lovely to share with you another beautiful time of fellowship. A friend loveth at all times. Thank the Lord for friends. Rose Mary.

August 8th 1981.

Many thanks for this cup of tea and all your interesting stories. Hope to see you again soon and wish you everything good. Patrice and Sandra.

November 18th 1983.

It was a very pleasant afternoon at your lovely home and above all for the nice fellowship. Prema Isaac. India.

November 11th 1983.

God bless you. Orpha Garrick. Mexico.

April 5th 1992.

So pleased to see you've got such a nice view. Michael [Chaplin].

Just a sample of 300 or so entries.

1985 dawned with lots of snow that prevented me from venturing out. Thank goodness for friends, they did my shopping and other odd jobs making life easy for me. On 21st January I was alone at home and thought of father; I sat down and cried a little, this was the date he died. If only things could have been different, Mother loved him very much. I never got over seeing them argue and the resultant unhappiness that it brought. I had resolved at that time never to marry if this was the result.

Lady Chaplin phoned to say that since her husbands death she was feeling very lonely and invited me to visit her whenever I was in Vevey. I should look upon the Manoir as my second home. I could not refuse such an invitation and called to see her on many future occasions.

Late March when I was feeling better I flew to London, staying at the Commonwealth Club, visited a Chagall and Renoir exhibition with Nennette, continued on to Bournemouth at the St Georges Hotel. Audrey picked me up and took me to her home where I visited most nearby relatives. On the 29th flew back home. A visit by Ann Hodgeson was not welcome as she was the worse for wear with drink. I wish she would not drink so much.

My very good friend Carmel was mourning the death of her companion Danny. She needed a lot of tender loving care. I invited her around for meals as this was easy as she only lived below me in the flats.

Judith came in to say her mother Nancy was very unwell. She was receiving treatment but was not responding. Two weeks later Judith said she feared the end was near and so it was, on 5th September. Nancy died. Oh dear! Every one of my dear friends seem to be leaving this world. I must enjoy life if I can.

The next few years were carried on as before with visiting friends for meals, inviting them to my flat for tea, going to the theatre or to a cinema if there was a good film on. I continued my trips to Vevey were almost every month, always staying at the Manoir or Les Avants with Ann Hodgeson. Audrey and Ken visited me every year.

My contacts with Lady Chaplin and the Sistovaris families continued to strengthen; they visited me regularly. I always wanted to know all the family news and to know where her children were and what they were doing. The years were punctuated with highlights such as the death of the Duchess of Windsor in Paris, the marriage of the Duke of York in London and the death of my friend Helen in Vancouver.

December 1st 1986. Today I am 80 years old. Thanks be to God.

Christmas with Mary Haour and family. I am very lucky to have such friends.

Opening my new diary I found an old Dutch saying, "Life must be understood backwards but lived forwards". That is good, I will try to do that.

KK had by now been admitted to a Nursing Home, as she could not look after herself. I visited her but she did not know me.

During April I did manage to go to London for the reunion of the pupils of my old school Balmoral Hall in Winnipeg. It was delightful, I was the oldest there, being year 1924. I was so proud of that.

As I said before my eyesight was getting worse because of cataracts. My Doctor arranged for me to go into hospital for their removal. I could not put this problem off any longer and went into the Geneva Hospital for an operation. I usually hate hospitals but I must admit my stay was pleasant and the actual operation not so terrible as I had imagined. The bill of course, was considerable.

December 1989 brought heavy snowfalls and it was during this time that KK died. She was my companion as governess for a very long time. We did everything together with the Chaplin children. We had lived in opposite rooms and were always together in the evenings after work with our usual whiskey. Lady Chaplin phoned to tell me the news and she was very sad. I also spoke to Eugene and reminisced about our escapades together. The next day being Sunday I did not manage Church, I could not face it I was so upset.

The next few months slipped by until Audrey and Ken came to see me in October on their way home from their holiday. They always came by car and suggested that if I was fit enough they would take me back to the U.K., if I wanted a little holiday. I jumped at the chance and set of with them to Auxerre where we put up for the night at a small hotel called "Maximes" overlooking the river Yonne.

We continued on and crossed the channel to Portsmouth. We were at Audreys home 30 minutes later. I stayed with them for 10 days, being waited on hand and foot. We visited lots of beautiful places in Hampshire and I was sure I benefited from the rest.

I returned home by air from Heathrow and settled down for more quiet days.

1991 seemed to me to bring further unpleasant news. The early part was pleasant but during September thing began to go wrong. First Annie phoned to talk about her life that was in turmoil; then came news that Lady Chaplin was not expected to live much longer, Jane and Josie both phoned me in great distress. We talked for ages. Several days latter she died. Vickie phoned me and cried all the time. October 1ˢᵗ was the funeral at Corsier. I went up to Vevey staying at the "Famille Hotel". After the service we all went back to the Manoir, where Mary had a buffet laid on. Well, here I was, the only remaining adult of the clan. My children were all about me and I loved them all. It was a sad occasion.

To cap it all Gerry Epstein died in America on the 21ˢᵗ November. He it was that helped Sir Charles with all his films and Music.

The year 1992 brought no unpleasant news but it was clear to me that I would be unable to manage my cooking and cleaning of my flat if my general health continued to get worse. I arranged for a nurse to visit me on a regular basis whilst my friends also helped me a lot but I could not rely on them all the time. I wrote to Audrey saying how I felt and to explore the possibility of my returning to the U.K. for the remainder of my life. She phoned me and wrote to me long letters discussing this proposal. Private nursing homes were very expensive. But above all if they were no more expensive than the ones in Switzerland, she might as well stay in Geneva where she had so many friends. In spite of my family being near to hand in England I would enjoy being in my usual environment in Geneva and perhaps going on her usual outings if she felt like it. This reasoning seemed sensible to me and after a little thought I decided to stay.

Meanwhile my friend Bobbie had had the same problem and she had found a nice new Nursing Home at Versoir, just outside Geneva. It was a very modern and nice establishment. I thought this would be ideal for me and arranged to go and stay there with Bobbie for a few days to get the feel of the place. I thought it was suitable and applied for a place as soon as possible.

The weeks and months went by in my usual routine, nothing particular happening. 1993 was calm and uneventful. My monthly prayer meetings were always welcomed and I met old and new friends who came to visit me in my flat and tell me about their lives. Always writing in my visitors book.

My health deteriorated but at the end of the year I was still in my flat. A room at the Nursing Home had not been available but they said maybe one would be available soon. I waited with hope. It was not until March 1994 that the "Bon Sejour Residence" informed me that a room would be ready for me on May 10th. This meant that I could take some of my furniture, but not all. I must clear my flat and dispose of all my other items. Audrey and Ken came to my rescue when they said they would come and do this for me. This they did and duly arrived staying at a flat at Corzent near Thonon in France (by kind invitation, of my good friend Judith Rickinson), that was only 30 miles away. They would stay there for two weeks to help me and then go on for a further two weeks on holiday elsewhere.

They came each day to do all the packing, putting everything in boxes and marking what it was. I had promised to give something to my best friends to remember me by and they came to collect these items during the week. All my kitchen utensils were given to the Red Cross for shipment to the Bosnian refugees. I was pleased about that. The furniture due to go to the Home was sent on ahead of me. The rest was dispatched as I wanted. Audrey and Ken took me to the Home and installed me, arranging my furniture as I desired. Then they returned to the flat to wash and clean everything , then they handed the keys over to the owners.

The Residence was modern, warm and very well run. Every other day I had a good bath given me by two nurses, followed by physio and exercises. The food was good but I was still able to go out to restaurants when friends called on me. My monthly trips with the Skylarks were a real treat, especially when we went on the lake in a steamer. I still had all my friends as Audrey had said, she was right to advise me to stay in Switzerland. I wrote and wrote to all my friends abroad, telling them of my present situation. Back came replies that I could barely keep up with.

Christmas came when I spent the day with all my fellow patients, with a special menu for lunch and carols afterwards by a local choir. I had a quick glass of whiskey up in my room.

The New Year came in very cold with thick snow. My room was warm but I was always somewhat uncomfortable. My eyes and legs continued to play me up and I realised I was getting weaker. My Doctor who visited me regularly changed my pills but to no avail; some days I felt terrible, others quite good. One thing I was pleased about was that my Chaplain, the Rev Kimber, at my old Church in Geneva came every two weeks to give me communion in my room. It gave me great confidence.

Audrey and Ken contacted me by phone on a regular basis, to inquire about my health. They became so alarmed at my failing health they arranged to come to see me during January. They stayed at the Novotel Hotel in Ferney, only 10 minutes away by car. I was feeling better one day when they called at the same time as Carmel. Carmel suggested we all should go out to a restaurant called "Chateaux de Perches" near the lake. The meal was good but getting my wheelchair into the car was almost impossible. That was a lovely interlude. February came and I was invited to a Church Luncheon in Geneva; as I was feeling quite well, I went. Had I known what would happen in the afternoon I would not have gone.

All the Chaplin children were due in Geneva for a meeting with their lawyers and to sign papers regarding the estate. They all decided to visit me, of course I was out.

They wrote a little message from each of them and left it for me.

What a shame we missed you Pinnie. Next time we are all together we will try and phone first. It will be by very soon for another visit. Love Michael.

Pinnie….. we [Michael, Josie, Annie and me] came to give you a surprise visit. But what a shame. We didn't phone cause we didn't know if we could make it. Love Geraldine.

Dear Pinnie. Sorry we missed you!!!!! But I am sure you're having a great lunch.

All my love sageterius pal. Annie.

Oh Pinnie. What a shame I missed you. But I hopefully will soon again. Much much love and kisses. Josie.

I was heart broken that I missed them and wrote to them all to say how sorry I was that I was out. The physio and exercises continued that kept me a little mobile. But I was feeling very frail when the doctor called, we talked and he gave me courage.

On Friday 10th February 1995 the Residence Bon Sejour telephoned Michael Chaplin to say that Pinnie was deteriorating fast and they considered he ought to come if he wished to see her before she passed away. Michael said he would go on Sunday 12th but his wife said he must go at once as it was most urgent.

Michael went to see her on the Saturday morning and found her asleep. After a few minutes she opened her eyes and recognised him. He held her hand and spoke calmly to her before she closed her eyes for the last time.

Audrey and I were at home on Saturday 11th February, preparing for a birthday party for my eldest son Julian on the following day. The telephone rang. It was the Residence Bon Sejour at Versoir to inform me that my Aunt had died that day.

It was my duty as Executor to implement her wishes as per her Will that was in my keeping. The Residence informed me that she had been removed to a Chapel of Rest in Geneva, pending further instructions knowing that I was her next of kin. My wife and I hastily made preparation to fly to Geneva on the Monday morning. Before long the phone rang again, it was Shirley Buchmann to offer her condolences and an offer to put us up at her house at Tannay if we were coming to Geneva. Bobbie had informed her of the death. We also had a call from Judith Rickinson expressing her sorrow at the news.

My wife and I arrived in Geneva as planned at lunchtime on Monday to be met by Shirley with a car to take us to her house. After lunch we went to the Residence to pick up her personal items and arranged for her furniture to be put in store there pending further plans. We than went on to the undertakers. A.Murith. S.A., where her body had been taken. They informed us that over forty people had visited them and signed the visitors condolence book that morning. More were expected in the next few days.

Mr Murith was a great help in advising us on the procedure common in Geneva as regards to funerals. A Notice was inserted in the evening paper to announce her death and that the funeral service would be held at the Holy Trinity Church, rue du Mont-Blanc on Wednesday 15th February at 11.00 hrs - to be conducted by the Rev Kimber.

Arrangements were made, as per her Will, for her body to be cremated in order that I could take her ashes to be buried with her mothers in Oxford, England.

Shirley taxied us all over Geneva including to the Notaire Monsieur Alfred Necker who was my fellow Executor. There we sorted her Will and made preparation to finalise her estate which would take some time.

Wednesday, the funeral day came quickly and Shirley and Martin her husband drove us to the Church. The Anglican Church in Geneva is exactly the same as any C of E Church in England. We felt quite at home. The Church quickly filled up with most of her friends and other people from all parts of the world whom she had befriended and entertained to tea. People from Africa were dressed in their finest coloured robes. I was told there were over three hundred people there. The flowers were absolutely beautiful, masses of them with special 2 metre wreaths from the Chaplin's and the Sistovaris families complete with a band giving their name. The service was the usual Anglican order with Psalm 23. Hymn, Abide with me. The Rev Kimber gave a special address as follows:-

ADDRESS

We are here today to give thanks to God for the life of Mabel Rose Pyniger, and to remember all that she meant to each of us, from so many walks of life and in so many ways. The fact that there are so many of you here, is a tribute to the number of lives she affected. However, only half of her days were spent here in Switzerland. She was born in Canada, and shaped in a special way by growing up and learning the Christian faith in that great country.

She was graced with an openness and generosity of spirit, and a capacity for friendship that enabled her to share richly with others the abundance of the love of God with which she knew she had been blessed. More than a decade, including the war years, spent in England helped to shape her destiny and prepare her to touch so many lives here. And not only the children she worked with as a governess, but also the adults in their lives, and in the life of this church community.

The great tolerance she displayed towards others was not born out of any incapacity to discriminate good from ill, but from a depth of love for others, as all-embracing as the love with which she knew, solidly and certainly, that God loved her. This knowledge born of faith was not something expressed in outward piety or religiosity, but in a character formed by divine graciousness. She had a strength and gentleness of spirit, that gave her a capacity to accept others unconditionally, and to understand them just as they are, with all their strengths and weaknesses- the light and the dark sides of their characters, just as God would.

It has been my privilege to become another of her friends in the past two years, during which she has struggled to accept growing weakness, given up her home and moved finally, happily, into the Residence Bon Sejour. Once it became too much of a trial to get to church regularly, I was able to take Holy Communion to her there, which was a great joy to her, but always an occasion when I felt ministered unto by her supportive interest and understanding, just as much as I was able to minister.

She loved this church, and it was marvellous that she was able to be here at lunch with many old friends in the Womens Guild, just two weeks ago today. Apparently she was disappointed [having used the outside lift instead of the stairs to go down to the Church Hall], not to be able to come in and look at the stained glass windows, something she cherished.

It was typical of her deep rooted Anglicanism- the traditional building where she felt so at home in personal and common prayer, her affection for its modern glass, bright, adventurous, abstract-symbolic, standing for an ancient faith in modern dress.

She was at home among people in todays world, but the values by which she lived, and shared Gods love with others, were rock solid and everlasting. There was in her this comprehension of other people, and attentiveness to their troubles, a deep wisdom and compassion, such as only comes from the heart of God, and triumph over personal suffering.

It was a privilege to be able to visit her and give her the last rites on the last day of her earthly life, and to know from all that we had shared, how much she treasured these moments of prayer, and looked forward happily to passing into the presence of our Heavenly Father. We give thanks for having known her and glimpsed in her divine grace at work. In all our sadness at losing such a good friend, we can sing "Alleluia". Because in her, there was real trust in the power of divine love, stronger than death, and the hope of resurrection to eternal life.

Rev Kimber.

And so the service ended. In the Church Hall under the Church, refreshments were provided by the Ladies of the Womens Guild. We mingled with the mourners and thanked them for coming. We cannot remember who most of them were but all of them without exception praised and remembered with affection their meetings with Pinnie.

The following day we returned to the Funeral Parlour to collect her ashes, and flew back to the U.K. Taking with us all her personal letters and diaries with which I was able write this story of her life. Two weeks latter I arranged another small church service for her relations and friends in England at the chapel at Wolvercote Cemetery, in the City of Oxford. Her ashes were interred with her mother and a stone was placed there to commemorate the event.

The compulsive traveller was now at last "Resting in Peace".

The End.

Extracts From Pinnies Visitors Book

Thank you for the hospitality! So glad you came to Holy Trinity.
Geneva.

Cynthia Cram.

What a difference it makes to have a good friend living so near.

Morvyth.

Muchas gracio par el trarajo que usted me da.

Veneda Caloagno

Thank you Mabel for such a happy, lovely early summer day with you in your beautiful flat.

Margaret Bedworth.

Mabel dear, all I can think to write is the Chinese wish on parting from a dear friend." Slowly slowly go. Quickly quickly come"

Turdi Bomba, Encino, California. May 1981.

Many thanks for this cup of tea and all your interesting stories. Hope to see you again soon and wish you everything good.

Patrice and Sandra.

It is not so easy to express my thanks for such a warm welcome and lovely stay, but I shall take away with me very happy memories of our friendship and your outstanding hospitality. Thank you with all my heart.

Phyllis. 04.12. 81.

So glad to have you in our sherry club.

Elizabeth Pellanda

What a lovely surprise to find such a lovely neighbour, thank you for your kind invitation today and I hope we shall meet again often.

Judith Rickinson.

So say I. Nancy Rickinson. 05.07.82.

Thank you.

Anne- Maria Pun-Myaing

10/ A. Short Street.

Sanchaung.

Rangoon. Burma.

Short visit, fun, Come back to Montreal as soon as you can.

All my love. Menk. 06.02.83.

So good to see you again, and know your kindness, Ian sends you his best love, remember you are always welcome in Canada.

Love, Anne and Krislina. Neva, Mt Martin. 83.

May God bless you and keep you in his loving arms always. Always remember, Just believe.

Mary Ann Odens. Washington. D.C. 11.11.83.

Thank you for the useful and wonderful time spent here studying the word of God and knowing his love and forgiveness, Thank you for this time of fellowship, God bless you. Mrs T Isaac. India.

Thank you Mabel for a lovely day, meeting you has made my holiday/

Kath Houghton. U.K.19.06.84.

It's been a lovely afternoon and as Charlie said I am happy to be here!

Hope to come back soon if you will have us again.

I love you. Vicky. 17.10.86

Haven't we had a lovely time this week. Vevey for three days, then France

Yesterday. Wish I didn't have to go back today. Many thanks for all your

Kindness. Love Nennette. 26.08.89.

Back again full of chat and heartache, your such a good listener.

Hopefully I'll be back for good in September and will have a good meal at

MacDonalds in the Rue du Mont Blanc. Thee and thy walking stick.

Take care. Love Sarah. 17.03.91.

About The Author:

Kenneth Parrett is now retired and had never written a book before and therefore cannot claim to be an established author.

The son of a tenant dairy farmer, he was born on 14th July, 1929. He was not a brilliant pupil at school and left at the age of 16 to join his father working a rural Farm. His life revolved around milk production and creating a modern Dairy processing milk for retail distribution.

His hobbies were painting landscapes in oil and foreign travel.

His holidays were spent touring the back roads of France and the mountains and Lakes of Switzerland. This was aided by his Canadian aunt, Mabel Pyniger, whom he visited at least twice a year as she lived in Switzerland at both Vevey and Geneva.

After Mabel's death Kenneth decided to write her life story. This entailed detailed research of her life in Canada, UK and Europe and was aided by extensive personal diaries that Mabel always kept up-to-date. Indeed they painted such fantastic relationships, situations and scenes that the reader can only be astounded as the story of her life unfolds before you.

Fact can be stranger than Fiction - as Mabel always said, Glory be!

She really did live a charmed life; one that Kenneth hopes may be inspirational to others.

ABOUT THE BOOK:

This book is the account of the life of a very remarkable woman.

Mabel was born in Winnipeg, Canada in 1906. Her father had a liking for alcohol and this drained the finances to an extent that resulted in hardship. Nevertheless, she received a good education; fees being paid by her mother undertaking dressmaking and by her uncle in London. Later she obtained a secretarial post with the Hydro Company in Winnipeg.

Her father died in 1929 leaving Mabel and her mother destitute. They then decided to return to England where they set up home in the east end of London where Mabel obtained employment with Spitalfield Market, near the docks.

Unfortunately they suffered the effects of two German bomb hits during the war that forced them to move out to Oxford. Mabel found employment in the Mayor's Office but then moved on to the University Employment Office.

Her mother died in 1949 leaving Mabel alone for first time in her life. She decided to travel the world and set off to tour Europe. She advertised herself as a Companion or Nanny and this resulted in employment in Belgium and then Switzerland where she worked for an Argentine family.

Her life moved onto a much higher level when she was offered a position with a certain **Charles Chaplin**. Together with another nanny, she was placed in charge of a family that was to increase year by year. She met many notable people from the film industry, politics and also Royalty from around the globe.

During her long stay in Europe everyone called her "Pinnie", being short for Pyniger, her surname.

The book takes the reader through her fascinating life-style finishing with a remarkable eulogy by the Vicar of the Holy Trinity in Geneva. She truly was "one of a kind".

Printed in the United Kingdom
by Lightning Source UK Ltd.
127847UK00001B/125/A